THE BIRTH OF THE CODEX

D1715181

THE BIRTH OF THE CODEX

COLIN H. ROBERTS

and

T. C. SKEAT

LONDON · *Published for* THE BRITISH ACADEMY
by THE OXFORD UNIVERSITY PRESS

*This book has been printed digitally and produced in a standard specification
in order to ensure its continuing availability*

OXFORD
UNIVERSITY PRESS

Great Clarendon Street, Oxford OX2 6DP

Oxford University Press is a department of the University of Oxford.
It furthers the University's objective of excellence in research, scholarship,
and education by publishing world-wide in

Oxford New York

Auckland Bangkok Buenos Aires Cape Town Chennai
Dar es Salaam Delhi Hong Kong Istanbul Karachi Kolkata
Kuala Lumpur Madrid Melbourne Mexico City Mumbai Nairobi
São Paulo Shanghai Taipei Tokyo Toronto

Oxford is a registered trade mark of Oxford University Press
in the UK and in certain other countries

Published in the United States
by Oxford University Press Inc., New York

© The British Academy 1983

The moral rights of the author have been asserted
Database right Oxford University Press (maker)

Reprinted 2004

All rights reserved. No part of this publication may be reproduced,
stored in a retrieval system, or transmitted, in any form or by any means,
without the prior permission in writing of Oxford University Press,
or as expressly permitted by law, or under terms agreed with the appropriate
reprographics rights organization. Enquiries concerning reproduction
outside the scope of the above should be sent to the Rights Department,
Oxford University Press, at the address above

You must not circulate this book in any other binding or cover
And you must impose this same condition on any acquirer

ISBN 0-19-726061-6

Antony Rowe Ltd., Eastbourne

CONTENTS

PREFACE

THE predecessor of this monograph, *The Codex*, was published in the *Proceedings of the British Academy*, 40 (1954), pp. 169–204 and was substantially based on two lectures delivered as the Special University Lectures in Palaeography at University College, London, in January 1953. When stock was exhausted, it was clear that in view of subsequent discoveries and further work on the subject more than a reprint was called for. Since at that time I was not free to undertake the revision myself, Mr T. C. Skeat generously agreed to do it on my behalf. The present book, a completely revised and in some respects enlarged version of its predecessor, is the result of his work; for the structure of the whole and the first seven Sections he is solely responsible. We have, however, collaborated throughout and the work as it stands represents our joint views.

Two books have greatly lightened our task, Sir Eric Turner's *The Typology of the early Codex* (University of Pennsylvania Press, 1977) and the Abbé Joseph van Haelst's *Catalogue des Papyrus Littéraires Juifs et Chrétiens* (Paris, 1976) and to their authors we wish to express our indebtedness.

C. H. Roberts

LIST OF ILLUSTRATIONS

INTRODUCTION

THE most momentous development in the history of the book until the invention of printing was the replacement of the roll by the codex; this we may define as a collection of sheets of any material, folded double and fastened together at the back or spine, and usually protected by covers. There has never been any doubt about the physical origin of the codex, namely that it was developed from the wooden writing tablet; there should have been little doubt about the time when this development took place, although it has needed the impact of successive discoveries, mainly but not entirely in Egypt, during the present century to induce scholars to take notice of what their literary authorities told them. But the questions why this change took place when it did, in what circles the codex was first used, and why it eventually supplanted the roll, are more complex and uncertain. The aim of the present work is to suggest at least provisional answers based upon a reappraisal of our literary sources coupled with an analysis of the evidence from papyri.

It is no part of the plan of this work to attempt to compile a bibliography of the vast literature (much of it now antiquated and inaccurate, or falsified by subsequent discoveries) concerning the codex, its origins and development. Any worker in this field must begin by expressing his obligations to Theodor Birt's *Das antike Buchwesen in seinem Verhältnis zur Literatur*, Berlin, 1882, supplemented many years later by his *Kritik und Hermeneutik nebst Abriss des antiken Buchwesens* (Iwan v. Müller, Handbuch der Altertumswissenschaft, I. Band, 3 Abt., München, 1913). As a collection of the literary material Birt's work is indispensable and calls for few supplements, but the eccentricity of its interpretations makes it an unsafe guide even to these sources. Much can be learned from W. Schubart's *Das Buch bei den Griechen und Römern* (2nd edition, Berlin, 1921; the so-called 3rd edition, by E. Paul, Heidelberg and Leipzig, 1961, though embellished with additional illustrations, omits the notes which are so valuable a feature of the 2nd edition), which still remains not only the most readable but also the most reliable introduction to the whole subject. There are many valuable observations in K. Dziatzko's *Untersuchungen über ausgewählte Kapitel des antiken Buchwesens*, Leipzig, 1900, supplemented by his articles 'Buch' and 'Buchhandel' in Pauly-Wissowa, *Real-Encyclopädie*. Considering the period when he wrote, Theodor Zahn's admirable treatment of the evidence for the Christian book in his *Geschichte des neutestamentlichen Kanons*, i, pp. 60 sq. (Berlin, 1888) is vitiated only by the then common assumption that papyrus implies the roll and parchment the codex. All these discussions, even to a large extent that of Schubart, were written before the full effect of the Egyptian discoveries had been appreciated, and these set the sources the authors quoted in a different light. A notable attempt to re-assess the question against the background of these discoveries is that of H. A. Sanders, *The Beginnings of the modern Book: the Codex*[1], University of Michigan Quarterly Review, 44, no. 15, Winter 1938, pp. 95–111, while among studies which have appeared since the first edition of the present work, mention may be made of H. Hunger, O. Stegmüller, and others, *Geschichte der Textüberlieferung der antiken und mittelalterlichen Literatur*, Zürich, 1961, especially pp. 47–51 (Hunger), 346–50 (K. Büchner). F. Wieacker, *Textstufen klassischer Juristen* (Abhandlungen der Akademie der Wissenschaften in Göttingen, Phil.-hist. Kl., 3. Folge, Nr. 45, 1960), especially in his §4, 'Rolle und Codex, Papyrus und Pergament', discusses the transition from roll to codex in relation to his principal thesis, namely that the works of the classical jurists (Ulpian, Paulus, etc.) were originally published in rolls, and were transferred to codices *circa* A.D. 300, and that hand in hand with this transference went a re-edition of the works themselves. Tönnes Kleberg, *Buchhandel und Verlagswesen in der Antike*, Darmstadt, 1969, includes (pp. 69–86) an *Exkurs über die Buchherstellung und die Formen des Buches in der Antike* which provides an excellent summary of the question. Sir Eric Turner's *The Typology of the early codex*, 1977, though a mine of information concerning all physical aspects of the codex, explicitly (cf. pp. 1–2) excludes any discussion of the origin of the codex form. The latest treatment, by Guglielmo Cavallo in his composite

---

[1] See also the articles of C. C. McCown, 'Codex and Roll in the New Testament', *Harvard Theological Review*, 34, 1941, pp. 219–50, and 'The earliest Christian books' in *The Biblical Archaeologist*, 6, 1943, pp. 21–31.

volume, *Libri, Editori e pubblico nel Mondo antico*, 1975, is considered in Section 12 below. It should be added that the task of assembling the data on texts other than Christian has been immeasurably lightened by the publication of Roger A. Pack, *The Greek and Latin Literary Texts from Greco-Roman Egypt*, University of Michigan Press, 1st edition 1952, 2nd edition 1965, here referred to as Pack[1] and Pack[2]. In the predecessor of the present work the evidence was based on Pack[1]; here it has been revised with the aid of Pack[2] and brought up to date with the aid of other bibliographies. For Christian texts the bibliographies of Kurt Aland and Joseph Van Haelst mentioned below (p. 38) have been of outstanding value.

This introductory section may suitably close with a warning. An overwhelming proportion of the evidence comes from Egypt, and even then not from the centre of literary and bibliographical studies, Alexandria, but from various provincial towns and villages.[1] The chances of such a limited field of discovery enjoin great caution, and we cannot assume that, for example, the proportions of rolls and codices, or of papyrus and parchment, which have survived from different periods, reflect the position in the ancient world generally. It is to some extent reassuring that, for instance, similarities can be traced between the finds at two different city-sites, Oxyrhynchus and Antinoë,[2] but these are less than 100 miles apart, and some correspondence would be expected. It is also reassuring that the statistics on pp. 36–7 below, based on Pack[2] with additions, reveal much the same position as those in the first edition of this work, based on Pack[1]. But it must be borne in mind that apart from a few isolated discoveries, the bulk of the additions come from the same sources as before, and indeed most of the additional Oxyrhynchus material was actually excavated even before the publication of Pack[1].

Two passages which sum up the difficulties and dangers in evaluating the material may be quoted here. The former is from T. Kleberg's *Buchhandel und Verlagswesen* mentioned above (p. 67):

---

[1] On the distribution of finds see E. G. Turner, *Greek Papyri*, 1968, Chapter IV: Place of Origin and Place of Writing; the Geographical distribution of Finds, pp. 42–53. The paperback edition of 1980 contains, on pp. 201–2, some supplementary notes. Over 50% of all literary papyri of known origin come from Oxyrhynchus, cf. P. Mertens, *Proceedings of the 12th International Congress of Papyrology*, pp. 303–4.

[2] Mertens, ibid., pp. 304–7.

'Diese Darstellung konnte nur einige bruchstückartige Züge aus
der Geschichte des antiken Buchhandels bieten. Aber wir müssen
tatsächlich feststellen, dass alles, was wir überhaupt von dieser
Einzelheit des antiken Lebens wissen, bruchstückartige Episoden
sind, die zusammengestellt, von verschiedenen Seiten aus
beleuchtet und durch nicht immer gleich gut begründete Schluss-
folgerungen ergänzt werden müssen. So steht es übrigens mit den
meisten Gebieten des antiken Alltagslebens. Die Schriftsteller der
Antike bieten uns äusserst selten vollständige zusammenhängende
Schilderungen. Meist müssen wir uns mit einzelnen spärlichen
Notizen begnügen, die sich über grosse Teile der erhaltenen
Literatur und in Inschriften verstreut finden.'[1]

The same point had been made long before, and even more
incisively, by Prof. F. Zucker in a review of K. Ohly's *Stichometrische
Untersuchungen* (*Gnomon*, 8, 1932, p. 384); 'Ich möchte überhaupt
grundsätzlich bemerken, dass wir im Buchwesen in weit grösserem
Ausmass als man vielfach anzunehmen scheint, auf die Erwägung
von Möglichkeiten angewiesen sind. Das Material ist gefährlich
ungleichmässig, in mancher Hinsicht überaus reich, in mancher
überaus dürftig. Vor allem muss man davor warnen, Lücken
unserer Kenntnis auf Grund gewisser allgemeiner Vorstellungen
auszufüllen, die uns selbstverständlich erscheinen.'

[1] A very similar warning is given by Schubart, *Das Buch*...[2], p. 36.

PAPYRUS AND PARCHMENT

As emphasised in the preceding section, the origin of the codex form of book is a question quite distinct from that of the material of which the book is composed. Throughout the whole of the period here studied papyrus and parchment were both, though in varying proportions, in common use, and although our story begins with the papyrus roll and ends with the parchment codex as the dominant form of book, there is no evidence whatever to indicate whether the change of material influenced the change of form, or *vice versa*. What is certain is that the papyrus roll, the papyrus codex, the parchment roll, and the parchment codex were all perfectly adequate and acceptable forms of book,[1] and each, in different areas and at different periods, remained in use for many centuries.

Nevertheless, since it has been seriously claimed that the increasing use of parchment in some way promoted the transition from roll to codex,[2] it seems desirable to consider briefly both these materials.

First, the sources of information. The history of papyrus from every aspect in the period which concerns us is amply covered by Naphtali Lewis, *Papyrus in Classical Antiquity* (Oxford, 1974), a new and enlarged edition of his well-known *L'Industrie du Papyrus dans l'Égypte gréco-romaine* (Paris, 1934). Until recently no similar study has been devoted to the history of parchment, but now a full-scale scientific and technical investigation is available in R. Reed, *Ancient Skins, Parchments and Leathers* (Seminar Press, 1972).[3] To complement this there is a useful collection of the historical and literary evidence in the University of California dissertation of Richard R. Johnson, *The Role of Parchment in Greco-Roman Antiquity*,

---

[1] It is, for instance, quite wrong to describe the papyrus codex as a 'Bastardform' (Wieacker, *op. cit.*, p. 100) or as a 'Surrogat' for the parchment codex (ibid., p. 97, n. 22).

[2] Even so relatively recent a work as that of E. Arns, *La Technique du Livre d'après S. Jérôme*, 1953, could state (p. 23, n.) 'Le codex est d'ordinaire en parchemin'.

[3] Cf. also the same writer's later publication, *The Nature and Making of Parchment*, 1975.

1968 (published by University Microfilms in both microfilm and xerox form).

One of Johnson's principal services is to collect and elucidate the confused and partly contradictory accounts of the 'invention' of parchment at Pergamum in the second century B.C. The 'invention' as such is baseless, since leather and parchment were certainly in common use in Western Asia much earlier, and Johnson also dismisses as absurd the statement that through jealousy of the growing Pergamene library the Ptolemies placed an embargo on the export of papyrus to Pergamum (how could they in fact have taken such a step while maintaining supplies to the rest of the Mediterranean world?), and concludes that what actually happened was that the Pergamene authorities were forced to fall back on parchment when Egyptian supplies of papyrus were interrupted during the invasions of Egypt by Antiochus Epiphanes (170–168 B.C.). It was during the same period that Pergamene scholars introduced the new material to Rome, where no doubt the shortage of papyrus was no less keenly felt.[1] This suggestion is of importance for our study, since it would help to explain the Roman development of the parchment notebook which will be considered in the next Section.[2]

To explain the eventual supersession of papyrus by parchment a number of reasons have been put forward, and although most of them have little bearing on the origin and development of the codex, they may be briefly considered here.

The comparative qualities of papyrus and parchment have often been compared, usually to the disadvantage of the former.[3] The durability of both under normal conditions is not open to

[1] In a subsequent publication, 'Ancient and Medieval accounts of the "Invention" of Parchment', *California Studies in Classical Antiquity*, 3, 1970, pp. 115–22, Johnson reproduces, sometimes verbatim, but with some rearrangement and additions, most of the material in pp. 22–49 of his dissertation, omitting, however, the lengthy refutation (pp. 25–32) of Reifferscheid's ascription to Suetonius of the account found in Isidore of Seville.

[2] There is, of course, no reason whatever for supposing that the parchment volumes in use at Pergamum were in codex form, as conjectured by Marquardt, *Privatleben der Romer*, ii, p. 819; they must certainly have been rolls, cf. H. Ibscher, p. 5 in the article cited in the next note, and Johnson, *op. cit.*, pp. 56–7.

[3] A notable exception is the article by H. Ibscher, 'Der Codex' in *Jahrbuch der Einbandkunst*, 4, 1937, pp. 3–15, in which he discusses (pp. 5–7) the relative durability of papyrus and parchment and concludes that, at any rate in the climatic conditions of Egypt, papyrus had the advantage. This may be true, but then these conditions are peculiar to Egypt.

doubt. Many instances of the long life of writings on papyrus could be quoted, but this is no longer necessary, since the myth that papyrus is not a durable material has at last been authoritatively and, one would hope, finally refuted by Lewis (*op. cit.*, pp. 60–1). At the same time Lewis finds no difficulty in dispelling another popular delusion, namely that papyrus was essentially a fragile and brittle material.[1] He demonstrates that it was in fact extremely strong and flexible. Wieacker's claim that parchment was preferred for the codex because papyrus was too brittle to fold is totally without foundation.

A further question which has often been fruitlessly debated is whether papyrus or parchment was the more costly material – fruitlessly because objective criteria are almost wholly lacking. Richard R. Johnson (*op. cit.*, pp. 113–17) quotes a number of earlier opinions,[2] but finally concludes that the question is both unanswerable and meaningless. The great difficulty is that we have no comparative figures for the cost of papyrus and parchment during the same period of time. Of the few certain prices of papyrus rolls collected by Lewis (*op. cit.*, pp. 131–4)[3] the latest (10 dr. 3 chalk.) is dated third century, but as the amount shows it must antedate the massive inflation which marked the latter part of the century. Conversely, the only certain price recorded for parchment is that given in Diocletian's Maximum Price Edict of A.D. 301;[4] and there is no way in which the one can be balanced against the other.

Despite all that has been said above, even the strongest supporters of papyrus would not deny that parchment of good

[1] Cf., e.g. Wieacker, *op. cit.*, p. 97, n. 22: 'da sich Papyrus schlecht falten lässt' or p. 99: 'das Papyrusblatt sich schwerer heften und, ohne zu brechen, in Lagen legen lässt'. [2] For further bibliography see Wieacker, *op. cit.*, p. 97, n. 22.

[3] For an attempt to determine the length of a standard papyrus roll, and thereby the approximate cost of papyrus, cf. T. C. Skeat, 'The Length of the standard papyrus roll and the Cost-advantage of the Codex', *Zeitschrift für Papyrologie und Epigraphik*, 45, 1982, pp. 169–75.

[4] Cf. Marta Giacchero, *Edictum Diocletiani et Collegarum*, 1974. The entry in question (7. 38) is mutilated, but has been plausibly restored to read: 'Membranario in quaternione pedali pergameni vel crocati (denarii) xl.' This is taken to mean that a quaternion or quire of eight leaves (= 16 pages) of parchment cost 40 denarii. We now know (*contra* N. Lewis, *L'Industrie du papyrus...*, pp. 154–60) that the Price Edict also included a section on papyrus (33, 1–4), but unfortunately only the heading, περὶ χαρτῶν, plus a few odd letters, is preserved. In P. Petaus 30 (second cent. A.D.) there is mention of the purchase of some μεμβράναι, but as we do not know what these were, how much parchment they contained, or whether they were blank or contained written texts, the price(?) of 100 dr for eight of them affords no evidence.

quality is the finest writing material ever devised by man. It is immensely strong, remains flexible indefinitely under normal conditions, does not deteriorate with age,[1] and possesses a smooth, even surface which is both pleasant to the eye and provides unlimited scope for the finest writing and illumination. Above all, it possesses one outstanding advantage over papyrus: whereas production of papyrus was limited to Egypt, parchment could be produced wherever the skins of suitable animals were available in sufficient quantity. The possible effect of this factor will be considered below.

Why, and when, parchment replaced papyrus is a complex question detailed discussion of which is outside the scope of this book. The manufacture of papyrus in Egypt continued right up to the twelfth century A.D.,[2] long after it had for practical purposes been replaced by parchment in both the Western and the Eastern worlds, so the disuse of papyrus cannot have been caused simply by the cessation of its production. The Arab conquest of Egypt in 641 has often been thought to have caused interruptions in the export of papyrus, but papyrus continued to reach even Western Europe long after this event,[3] and in any case the gradual replacement of papyrus by parchment had begun much earlier.

As already mentioned, parchment had the advantage over papyrus in that it could be manufactured virtually anywhere. At first sight this advantage would seem to be so overwhelming that one is inclined to pose the question, not in the form 'Why did parchment replace papyrus?', but rather 'Why did parchment take so long to replace papyrus?' Here there is a technological factor which has not hitherto been sufficiently appreciated. Whereas the manufacture of papyrus, like that of paper, is basically a simple and straightforward process, and the technical skills necessary had in any case been elaborated by the Egyptians over thousands of years, the production of parchment poses very different problems, the nature of which can best be illustrated by the following quotations from R. Reed, *Ancient Skins, Parchments and Leathers*:

'It is perhaps the extraordinarily high durability of the product, produced by so simple a method, which has prevented most people from

[1] Cf. Pliny, N.H. 13, 70, describing parchment as 'rei qua constat immortalitas hominum'. [2] Lewis, *op. cit.*, pp. 92, 94, n. 10.
[3] Cf. Lewis, *op. cit.*, pp. 90–4, and the article by E. Sabbe, 'Papyrus et parchemin au haut moyen âge', *Miscellanea historica in honorem Leonis van der Essen*, i, 1947, pp. 95–103.

suspecting that many subtle points are involved.... The essence of the parchment process, which subjects the system of pelt to the *simultaneous* action of *stretching* and *drying*, is to bring about peculiar changes quite different from those applying when making leather. These are: (1) reorganisation of the dermal fibre network by stretching, and (2) permanently setting this new and highly stretched form of fibre network by drying the pelt fluid to a hard, glue-like consistency. In other words, the pelt fibres are *fixed in a stretched condition* so that they cannot revert to their original relaxed state' (pp. 119–20).[1]

'Where the medieval parchment makers were greatly superior to their modern counterparts was in the control and modification of the ground substance in the pelt, before the latter was stretched and dried.... The major point, however, which modern parchment manu-facturers have not appreciated is what might be termed the integral or collective nature of the parchment process. The bases of many different effects need to be provided for *simultaneously*, in one and the same operation. The properties required in the final parchment must be catered for at the wet pelt stage, for due to the peculiar nature of the parchment process, once the system has been dried, any after-treatments to modify the material produced are greatly restricted.' (p. 124).

'This method, which follows those used in medieval times for making parchment of the highest quality, is preferable for it allows the grain surface of the drying pelt to be "slicked" and freed from residual fine hairs whilst stretched upon the frame. At the same time, any processes for cleaning and smoothing the flesh side, or for controlling the thickness of the final parchment may be undertaken by working the flesh side with sharp knives which are semi-lunar in form.... To carry out such manual operations on wet stretched pelt demands great skill, speed of working, and concentrated physical effort.' (pp. 138–9).

'Enough has been said to suggest that behind the apparently simple instructions contained in the early medieval recipes there is a wealth of complex process detail which we are still far from understanding. Hence it remains true that parchment-making is perhaps more of an art than a science.' (p. 172).

From these statements it will be clear that a parchment industry on a scale adequate to enable it to challenge the

[1] In *The Nature and Making of Parchment*, pp. 43–4, Reed conjectures that the innovation of the Pergamenes consisted in the discovery that 'by simplifying the composition of the pelt preparation bath, allied with a special mode of drying wet unhaired pelts (by stretching them as much as possible) smooth taut sheets of uniform opacity could easily be obtained'.

dominance of papyrus could not have been created overnight. Many years – perhaps even centuries – would have been required to work out the details of the process by trial and error, and to build up and train a sufficient labour force spread over the length and breadth of the Roman Empire. We must also bear in mind the probable nature and size of the opposition which it had to face. Although our knowledge of the subject is virtually a blank, it is obvious that the organisation of the manufacture and distribution of papyrus must have been on a gigantic scale, involving many thousands of persons and supported by massive amounts of invested capital. This alone would have provided a formidable obstacle to any potential competitor, especially when backed by the natural conservatism of the public and popular reluctance to abandon a traditional and well-tried material. When we add to all this the technological difficulties already mentioned, it can readily be understood why the change-over took centuries to complete.

This brief survey will, it is hoped, be sufficient to show that the transition from papyrus to parchment was of an entirely different character from, and quite unconnected with, the transition from roll to codex, to which we will now turn.

3

THE WRITING TABLET

THE writing tablet need not long detain us. It was commonly formed of two or more flat pieces of wood, held together either by a clasp or by cords passed through pierced holes; the central area of the tablet was usually hollowed slightly to receive a coating of wax, while a small raised surface was often left in the centre to prevent the writing on the wax being damaged when the tablet was closed. Writing in ink or chalk was sometimes placed directly on the wood. It was one of the oldest, if not the oldest,[1] recipient of writing known to the Greeks, who may have borrowed it from the Hittites.[2] Homer knew of it, for it was on a folded tablet or diptych that Proitos scratched the 'deadly marks' (Iliad vi. 168 sq.) that were intended to send Bellerophon to his death. To the Greeks of the classical age the tablet had a tradition behind it and a dignity that the papyrus roll lacked;[3] in Sophocles, Agamemnon orders the muster roll of the Greek princes to be read from a tablet, and it is on a tablet that Zeus, in a fragment of Euripides, records the sins of men.[4] In later Greece they were the familiar recipient of anything of an impermanent nature – letters, bills, accounts, school exercises, memoranda, a writer's first draft. Already in the

[1] The Mycenaean Greeks, of course, used clay tablets and also, possibly, papyrus (cf. clay sealings containing impressions of papyrus fibres, Marinatos, *Minos*, i, p. 40; M. Pope, *Annual of the British School at Athens*, 55, 1960, p. 201), but neither seems to have survived the collapse of Mycenaean civilisation.

[2] See C. Wendel, *Die griechisch–römische Buchbeschreibung verglichen mit der des Vorderen Orients*, 1949, p. 91. A Western Asiatic origin is suggested also by the set of ivory tablets from Nimrud, dated to about 707–705 B.C.; these, which still retained some of their yellow wax coating, had originally been hinged together on both sides so as to fold up concertina-fashion, whereas the tablets of walnut wood found with them had perforations so that they could have been strung together by, e.g. leather thongs (*Iraq*, 16, 1954, pp. 65, 97–9; 17, 1955, pp. 3–20). For representations of wooden writing-tablets in Neo-Hittite reliefs of the same period see B. Regemorter, *Scriptorium*, 12, 1958, pp. 177 ff., ('Le codex relié à l'époque néo-Hittite').

[3] On this see Dziatzko, *op. cit.*, p. 138, quoting a paper by Fr. Marx (not accessible to us); the gods are represented as using δέλτοι, διφθέραι, ὄστρακα, σκυτάλαι, anything in fact except βίβλοι, the written papyrus roll. Cf. L. Koep, *Das himmlische Buch in Antike und Christentum*, 1952, pp. 15–16.

[4] Sophocles, fr. (Pearson) 144; Euripides, fr. 506 (Nauck).

fifth century tablets of several leaves were in use,[1] but the nature of the material would set a limit to their number, and in fact no specimen surviving from antiquity has more than ten.[2] The earliest surviving Greek tablets, seven in number, date from the middle of the third century B.C. All surfaces were covered with wax, sometimes black, sometimes red; they contain rough accounts of expenses during a journey on the Nile.[3] In Rome they were equally familiar from an early date and were employed not only for the casual purposes of everyday life but for legal documents and official certificates. Of their use as the author's notebook Pliny the Younger gives a vivid picture in his account of his uncle at work.[4] By his side stood a slave with a book to read to his master and tablets on which to take down in shorthand anything that had to be extracted or noted; from these tablets (*pugillares*) were compiled the immense *commentarii*, filling 160 rolls and written on both sides of each roll in a minute hand. These rolls must have been inconceivably cumbrous to use, particularly in the composition of a work such as the *Natural History*, and it is odd that, with the tablets at his side to point the way, Pliny did not anticipate the invention of the codex by substituting for the opisthograph roll a collection of folded sheets of papyrus.

The correct designation in Latin for a plurality of tablets or for multi-leaved tablets was *codex*, whether the material used was wood, as was usual or, e.g., ivory. When Seneca enlarges[5] on that *inane studium supervacua discendi*, an infection the Romans had contracted from the Greeks, he cites as an example the enquiry

---

[1] Cf. Euripides, *I.T.* 727, δέλτου μὲν αἴδε πολύθυροι διαπτυχαί. Schubart's comment (*op. cit.*, p. 175) that πτυχή is not strictly applicable to a hard material such as wood, and that therefore in this passage it implies a previous use of folded leather, papyrus, etc., is misconceived, since πτυχή can be used of the folds of doors. Cf. *LSJ* and Pollux, *Onomast.*, ed. Bethe, i, p. 207: καὶ Ἡρόδοτος μὲν λέγει 'δελτίον δίπτυχον', οἱ δ' Ἀττικοί, 'γραμματεῖον δίθυρον', καὶ θύρας τὰς πτύχας ἄχρι δύο, εἶτα πτυχὰς καὶ τρίπτυχον καὶ πολύπτυχον.

[2] For the uses to which tablets were put see Schubart, *Das Buch...*[2], pp. 24 sqq., and notes, p. 175; the ninefold wax tablet illustrated on p. 24 must originally have had ten leaves (see Plaumann's article referred to by Schubart, p. 175). P. Fouad 74 of the fourth century A.D. refers to and describes a δελτάριον δεκάπτυχον.

[3] Published by H. I. Bell and Flinders Petrie, *Ancient Egypt*, 3, 1927, pp. 65–74. For photographs of three of them see Petrie, *Objects of daily life*, pl. lix. One is reproduced here as Plate 1.

[4] *Ep.* iii. 5. 15 sq.

[5] *De Brevitate Vitae* 13. Seneca's account may derive from Varro *ap.* Nonius Marcellus p. 535 M (*quod antiqui pluris tabulas coniunctas codices dicebant*); cf. Seneca, *Contr.* i, praef. 18.

whether Claudius Caudex, one of the consuls of 264 B.C., was so called 'quia plurium tabularum contextus caudex apud antiquos vocabatur, unde publicae tabulae codices dicuntur.' Already in the time of Cato the Censor[1] the words *tabulae* and *codex* were interchangeable, and both are frequently found in Cicero for tablets used for business purposes.[2] But neither now nor for a long time to come was there any question of the word *codex* denoting a book.

Two passages which have been claimed as evidence for the use of parchment in codex form during the Republican period may be briefly considered here. At the funeral of Clodius in 52 B.C. the mob broke into the Senate House and piled up wooden furniture and *codices librariorum* to form a funeral pyre, which burned so fiercely that the Senate House itself was consumed. Schubart in discussing this passage strangely concludes that these *codices* were volumes of the official *Acta* of the Senate (*Aktenbände*), and implies, though he does not specifically say so, that they were on parchment. There is no evidence whatever for this hypothesis, and indeed no reason to suppose that *codices* in this passage had any other than its then normal significance of sets of waxed tablets.[3] As Sanders pointed out,[4] they were seized upon by the mob precisely because, like the wooden furniture, they were highly inflammable, whereas parchment is not inflammable and burns only with difficulty.[5]

The second passage, on which much ink has been spilt to little profit, is the statement by the elder Pliny that Cicero had reported a copy of the Iliad on parchment which could be enclosed in a

---

[1] Cato *ap.* Fronto, *Ep. ad Ant.* i 2, p. 99 N: *iussi caudicem proferri ubi mea oratio scripta erat...tabulae prolatae.*

[2] G. E. M. de Ste Croix, 'Greek and Roman Accounting' in *Studies in the History of Accounting*, ed. A. C. Littleton and B. S. Yamey, 1956, pp. 41–3; P. Jouanique, 'Le codex accepti et expensi chez Cicéron', *Revue historique de Droit français et étranger*, 46, 1968, pp. 5–31.

[3] For the view that the official records of the Senate were on wood or waxed tablets see e.g. G. Cencetti, 'Gli archivi dell' antica Roma nell' età repubblicana', *Archivi d' Italia*, Ser. 2, vii, 1940, p. 14, n. 29.

[4] 'Codices Librariorum', *Classical Philology*, 29, 1934, pp. 251–2, and 'The Codex', pp. 98–9. The same view is taken by E. Kornemann, art. 'Tabulae Publicae' in Pauly-Wissowa, *RE*; R. R. Johnson, *op. cit.*, pp. 65–6; E. Posner, *Archives in the Ancient World*, pp. 162–3; N. Lewis, *Bulletin of the American Society of Papyrologists*, 11, 1974, pp. 49–51.

[5] For the effect of heat on parchment see R. Reed, *Ancient Skins, Parchments and Leathers*, pp. 316–18.

nut (*in nuce inclusam Iliadem Homeri carmen in membrana tradit Cicero*).
This is quoted by Pliny (*N.H.* vii. 21. 85) to illustrate a case of
extremely good eyesight. It has often been denounced as an
absurdity.[1] Sanders, for instance,[2] sarcastically remarks that to
contain a manuscript of the entire Iliad the nut must have been
a coconut. He then attempts to rationalise the story by suggesting
that *in nuce*, instead of meaning 'in a nut-shell', could also mean
'in boards of nut-wood', i.e. the manuscript must have been a
codex bound in boards of a wood such as walnut. Bilabel, art.
Membrana in Pauly-Wissowa, *RE*, takes much the same line,
suggesting a box of nut-wood. However, as has been justly pointed
out, if *in nuce* does *not* mean 'in a nut-shell', the whole story loses
its point.

The trouble is that none of the scholars who have commented
on this passage have investigated the subject of microscopic
writing, and therefore have no conception of what can be
achieved by ingenuity and application. To take but a single
example, Harley MS. 530 in the British Museum contains (f. 14b)
a contemporary account of a Bible written by the celebrated
Elizabethan writing-master Peter Bales so small that it could be
contained in a walnut-shell. If Peter Bales could put the entire
Bible into a walnut-shell in the sixteenth century A.D. there seems
no reason why the much shorter Iliad[3] could not have been
similarly accommodated in the first century B.C. But in reality the
whole story is of no practical importance; it is simply one of the
'curiosities of literature'[4] and should not feature in any serious
discussion of either the employment of parchment[5] or the origin
of the codex. The attention which has been paid to this
trifling anecdote demonstrates only one thing – the extraordinary
poverty of our sources of information.

[1] Cf., e.g. R. R. Johnson, *op. cit.*, pp. 66–8.

[2] *The Codex...*, pp. 103–4.

[3] Very approximately, the Bible is six times as long as the Iliad.

[4] Isaac D'Israeli, *Curiosities of Literature*, 1881–2 edition, pp. 99–100. D'Israeli quotes
the story of the Peter Bales Bible as an example of minute writing, and then goes on
to discuss the Pliny passage, remarking that three centuries earlier the scholar Pierre
Daniel Huet had demonstrated that it was perfectly possible to write a copy of the Iliad
small enough to go in a walnut-shell.

[5] The choice of parchment rather than papyrus was no doubt dictated by the fact
that parchment can be pared down to any thinness required, whereas the thickness of
papyrus is unalterable. Sanders appears to assume that the manuscript was a codex,
but an opisthograph roll would have occupied less space and fitted better inside a
nut-shell.

4

FROM WRITING TABLET TO PARCHMENT
NOTE-BOOK

IT would seem that it was the Romans, rather than the Greeks, who developed the writing tablet to a size where it could accommodate lengthy accounts (they distinguished, as the Greeks did not, between the large tablet and the *pugillares* that could be held in a closed hand). Certainly it was the Romans who took the decisive next step, that of replacing the wooden tablet by a lighter, thinner and more pliable material. We have seen that, according to our literary evidence, the Romans may have been made familiar with parchment as a writing material before the middle of the second century B.C. But if, as also our sources suggest, it was intended as a substitute for papyrus, it would probably have been used, like papyrus, in roll form.[1] In any case it is probable that after the temporary interruption of supply papyrus regained its former predominance, though some knowledge of the usability of parchment may have subsisted.[2]

Evidence from the last years of the Republic is scanty and of doubtful interpretation. We have already dismissed the suggestion that the *codices librariorum* which contributed to the funeral pyre of Clodius were of parchment. A letter of Cicero to Atticus, written in 45 B.C., contains the sentence 'Quattuor διφθέραι sunt in tua potestate', and it has been conjectured that these parchments were in the form of rolls; but there is so much uncertainty about the interpretation of the passage that it cannot safely be used as evidence.[3] All we can perhaps infer is that Cicero's use of the Greek word διφθέραι indicates that although the use of parchment as a writing material was known in cultured

[1] Cf. p. 6 note 2 above.

[2] Apart from the Pergamene experiments, parchment was certainly being used in Priene in the first century B.C., cf. the inscriptions discussed by R. R. Johnson, *op. cit.*, pp. 57–9. These relate to the writing of local records in dual form, ἐν δερματίνοις καὶ βυβλίνοις τεύχεσιν. Did the official Zosimus, whose initiative is commemorated, appreciate the superior lasting quality of parchment later emphasised by Pliny?

[3] *Ad Atticum* xiii, 24, 1. Cf. D. R. Shackleton Bailey, *Cicero's Letters to Atticus*, vol. v, no. 332, and commentary pp. 379, 380.

Roman society, it was not sufficiently familiar for it to have a recognised Latin equivalent.

Another passage which has often been quoted in this connection is Catullus xxii, 4–8:

> puto esse ego illi milia aut decem aut plura
> perscripta, nec sic ut fit in palimpsesto
> relata: cartae regiae, novi libri,
> novi umbilici, lora rubra, membrana
> derecta plumbo, et pumice omnia aequata.

There are a number of textual problems in these lines, but these do not concern us here. There can at least be little doubt about the significance of *membrana* in l. 7: it is the parchment wrapper used to protect the papyrus roll. Controversy has however raged about the meaning of 'in palimpsesto'. It has, for instance, been argued that 'palimpsest' means 'scraped again', as in the case of parchment manuscripts of later centuries from which the original writing has been removed to enable the material to be re-used; and that since such vigorous action could not have been safely applied to a delicate material like papyrus, the term 'palimpsest' implies the use of parchment.

There is much misconception here. In the first place, the Greek form of the word shows that it was invented in an area of Greek culture, where papyrus would have been the normal writing material, and that the term must have applied, originally at any rate, to papyrus and not parchment. This is confirmed by the statement of Plutarch,[1] that Plato compared Dionysius of Syracuse to a βιβλίον παλίμψηστον, because traces of the tyrant showed through the veneer of refinement just as traces of earlier writing might remain in a papyrus roll from which the text had been washed off. Another passage in Plutarch,[2] ὥσπερ παλίμψηστα διαμολύνοντες, is less illuminating, but is also likely to refer to papyrus, since there is nothing to suggest parchment. Finally, the word recurs in Latin dress in a letter of Cicero: *nam quod in palimpsesto, laudo equidem parsimoniam; sed miror quid in illa chartula fuerit.*[3] Here the 'palimpsest' is unquestionably of papyrus, since it is equated with the following *chartula*.[4]

Thus all the evidence points to the conclusion that a 'palimpsest'

---

[1] *Moralia* 779 C.   [2] *Moralia* 504 D.
[3] *Ad fam.* vii. 18. 2.   [4] Cf. R. R. Johnson, *op. cit.*, pp. 60–1.

was a papyrus from which the writing had been removed to enable it to be re-used.

The second misconception concerns what may for convenience be termed the palimpsesting process. As Birt showed,[1] the verb ψάω does not necessarily connote anything so vigorous as 'scraping'; it means in fact nothing more than 'smoothing' or 'rubbing' which would be quite appropriate to the action of washing off the writing from papyrus with a sponge or cloth. Indeed, even in the case of parchment palimpsests of later ages the process was by no means so drastic as is commonly supposed: to quote E. A. Lowe,[2] 'The word *palimpsest* comes, as everyone knows, from the Greek παλίνψηστος, meaning scraped or rubbed again. Although the word enjoys general favour, it can be misleading. For one thing, the membranes of the palimpsests treated here were usually not subjected to a second scraping; the process was the more gentle one of washing off their original writing. It would be very difficult, if not impossible, to resuscitate the lower script if the membranes had been scraped again as thoroughly as they had been the first time...' Independent evidence of the nature of the palimpsesting process applied to papyrus is provided by a recipe in the Papyrus Holmiensis (ed. O. Lagercrantz, 1913), γ, ll. 18–29. This recipe is for a kind of paste intended primarily for whitening pearls, but which can also be used for removing writing from papyrus: αὕτη δὲ καὶ χάρτας γεγραμμένους πάλιν ψᾷ, ὥστε δοκεῖν μηδέποτε γεγράφθαι κτλ...ἐὰν δὲ εἰς χάρτην, μόνα τὰ γράμματα χρῖε. As Lagercrantz points out in the notes (pp. 160–1), 'Die Wörterbücher geben ψῶ wieder durch "kratze, reibe, streiche". Für unsere Stelle muss die Bedeutung "säubere" vorausgesetzt werden, und zwar so dass die Art und Weise, wie die Säuberung geschieht, ganz in den Hintergrund tritt. Durch Kratzung lässt sich Schrift auf Pergament, Wachs, usw. tilgen. Aber nicht auf Papyrus, der zu spröde ist, um eine Behandlung dieser Art vertragen zu können. Papyrus wird hingegen in der Regel gewaschen – πάλιν ist streng genommen tautologisch.' Although Lagercrantz does not enlarge upon his final observation, that πάλιν is tautologous, there can be little doubt that πάλιν ψᾷ (which might even be written παλιμψᾷ) is the verb of which παλίμψηστος

---

[1] *Kritik und Hermeneutik*, p. 290; cf. R. R. Johnson, *op. cit.*, p. 61.
[2] 'Codices Rescripti: a list of the oldest Latin palimpsests with stray observations on their origin', E. A. Lowe, *Palaeographical Papers*, ii, pp. 480–519.

is the verbal adjective. We could thus translate 'This (recipe) can also be used for palimpsesting written papyrus rolls' etc.

However, by far the greatest source of confusion has been the employment by modern palaeographers of the convenient term 'palimpsests' or its factitious Latin equivalent 'libri rescripti' to denote re-written *parchment* manuscripts, with the result that the word 'palimpsest' has become inextricably linked with the use of parchment, in defiance of all the ancient evidence. This misconception has coloured all discussion of the Catullus passage down to the present day.

This lengthy digression has been necessary to demonstrate that the Catullus passage has nothing to do with the use of parchment for writing material – let alone a parchment note-book, which for Suffenus's poem, which ran to over 10,000 lines and would thus have filled three papyrus rolls of normal size, would have been hopelessly inadequate. All the passage tells us is that it was normal practice (*ut fit*) for an author to use old papyrus rolls from which the text had been washed off for his own draft.[1] For publication this would, of course, be handed over to the scriveners for professional copying. Catullus here hits at the ridiculous vanity of Suffenus, who insisted on using only the finest materials for this first and transitory stage of composition.

One further passage which may be relevant for the writing practices of Republican Rome occurs in Suetonius, *Divus Julius*, 56, 6,[2] where he describes the form of Julius Caesar's despatches to the Senate in the following words: *Epistulae quoque eius ad Senatum extant, quas primum videtur ad paginas et formam memorialis libelli convertisse, cum antea consules et duces non nisi transversa charta scriptas mitterent.* Unfortunately the sense of the passage is far from clear. The first problem is to determine the form of writing used by Caesar's predecessors, from which his innovation constituted a departure. Suetonius describes these earlier despatches as '*transversa charta scriptas*'. Dziatzko,[3] followed by Maunde Thompson,[4] suggested that this meant written at right angles to the length of the roll (and therefore parallel with its axis). It has

[1] So R. Quinn, *Catullus: the Poems*, 1973, pp. 157–8 correctly translates it 'second-hand papyrus'.
[2] See C. H. Roberts, 'A Note on Suetonius, *Divus Julius* 56, 6', *J.R.S.* 23, 1933, pp. 139–42; Sanders, *The Codex*, p. 102.
[3] *Op. cit.*, p. 124.
[4] *An Introduction to Greek and Latin Palaeography*, 1912, p. 46, n. 3.

been objected that although such a manner of writing is found occasionally in Ptolemaic papyri of the third century B.C.[1] and again in papyri of the Byzantine age, there are no examples of either literary or documentary papyri so written from the intervening period. Nevertheless it now seems to be agreed[2] that this is the only possible interpretation of *transversa charta*, particularly as the only alternative, *viz.* with lines written parallel to the length of the roll, would simply be the normal method of writing and would require no special description. We now have to decide the nature of Caesar's innovation. In the first place his writing was certainly in a succession of columns, since this is the only possible meaning of *paginas*. Suetonius has thus adequately described the *method* of writing, and he now turns to the format (*ad formam*). It has been claimed that this form was simply the normal papyrus roll; but if so, why did Suetonius find it necessary to employ the unusual expression *memorialis libelli*?[3] If he had meant written in ordinary book form[4] he would presumably have said simply *ad formam libri*. If, on the other hand, *memorialis libri* means 'note-book' or, more literally, 'memorandum-book', we may conjecture that Caesar fastened a number of sheets together, like the parchment note-books (*membranae*) of which we shall hear later. If it is objected that in such a case Suetonius might have been expected to write *ad formam membranarum*, this might have been confusing since Caesar undoubtedly used papyrus, like his predecessors (*transversa charta*): Suetonius says that Caesar changed the *form* of his despatches, not the *material*.[5]

That Julius Caesar may have been the inventor of the codex (and, at that, of the papyrus codex) is indeed a fascinating proposition; but in view of the uncertainties surrounding the passage it is doubtful whether any such conclusion can be drawn.

---

[1] For the Ptolemaic evidence see J. Vergote, *Le Muséon*, 59, 1946, pp. 253–8.

[2] See most recently E. G. Turner, *The terms Recto and Verso: the Anatomy of the Papyrus Roll* (Papyrologica Bruxellensia 16), 1978, pp. 27–32.

[3] The examples quoted in the *Oxford Latin Dictionary*, s.v. *memorialis*, do not contribute anything positive to the interpretation of the phrase *memorialis libelli*.

[4] As concluded by J. Vergote, *op. cit.*, and F. G. Kenyon, *Books and Readers in Ancient Greece and Rome*, 2nd ed., 1951, p. 57, n. 1. This is also the position which E. G. Turner, *op. cit.*, p. 32, is 'inclined to prefer'.

[5] Sanders (*op. cit.*, p. 102) believed that Caesar used parchment, but there is no evidence whatsoever for this, and apart from Suetonius's wording, the Roman army's consistent use of papyrus over the centuries is against it.

Passing on to the Augustan age we reach firmer ground with two quotations from Horace:

Sic raro scribis, ut toto non quater anno
membranam poscas, scriptorum quaeque retexens (Sat. ii. 3, 1–2)

Si quid tamen olim
scripseris, in Maeci descendat iudicis auris
et patris et nostras, nonumque prematur in annum,
membranis intus positis: delere licebit
quod non edideris (Ars Poetica, 386–390)

We can see that by this time it was a well-established practice to use parchment for rough drafts of literary works. We can also conclude, from the reference to deletion in the second passage, that parchment was employed for this purpose because it possessed the same advantage of re-usability as waxed or wooden tablets, since the ink could easily be washed off the parchment.[1] Although there is no direct evidence at this period that these *membranae* consisted of sheets of parchment sewn or fastened together in what we may now call codex form, this is highly probable in view of the fact that they appear as alternatives to the waxed tablet. But it is not until late in the first century A.D. that this probability becomes a certainty, as will be shown below. In any case, we can see that already by the time of Horace a differentiation had arisen between the singular *membrana*, meaning the material, and the plural *membranae*, meaning the parchment note-book.

The story of the parchment note-book is continued in the first century A.D. by a quotation from Persius (*circ.* A.D. 55–60), when he lists the items needed by the student:

iam liber et positis bicolor membrana capillis
inque manus chartae nodosaque venit harundo (Sat. iii. 10–11)

Positis capillis clearly refers to the depilation of the skin in the process of parchment making. *Bicolor* is more difficult to interpret, but probably refers to the difference in colour between the flesh-side of parchment and the hair-side, which is often markedly

---

[1] This would be particularly easy with the carbon ink then in use, which has poor adhesion to parchment, cf. R. R. Johnson, *op. cit.*, pp. 102–3, 109–10. The earliest example of metallic ink in the Graeco-Roman world is perhaps P. Oxy. xliv. 3197, dated A.D. 111 (cf. P. Oxy. xliv, p. 169, n.).

yellower.[1] This difference would not leap to the eye in the case
of a parchment roll, in which all the membranes would be sewn
together the same way round, but it would be very noticeable in
the case of a parchment note-book in codex form, particularly if
care had not been taken to arrange the leaves so that flesh- and
hair-sides faced each other. The passage may thus be taken to
indicate that the *membranae*, at this period if not earlier, were
parchment note-books in codex form.

The final proof is provided by Quintilian (*circ.* A.D. 90), who
gives the following advice: *Scribi optime ceris, in quibus facillima est
ratio delendi, nisi forte visus infirmior membranarum potius usum exiget... re-
linquendae autem in utrolibet genere contra erunt vacuae tabellae, in quibus
libera adiciendi sit excursio.*[2] Here the allusion to the wax tablet and
the blank pages show that the codex form was in question. With
Quintilian we have reached a stage in the history of the codex
when it is more than a tablet but still less than a book.

Independent confirmation of the same trend comes from the
evidence of contemporary legal writers. Ulpian, in a passage
which will be discussed in detail below (p. 30) quotes an opinion
of Gaius Cassius, the jurisconsult who was Consul in A.D. 30 and
died under Vespasian, regarding legacies of books: *Gaius Cassius
scribit deberi et membranas libris legatis.* The *membranae* to which he
refers are no doubt the writer's note-books, and the *et* indicates
that their status was still far removed from the proper book, i.e.
the papyrus roll. The second piece of evidence is a citation in the
Digest to the *liber sextus membranarum* of the jurist Neratius Priscus,
a contemporary of Trajan.[3] Some scholars have thought to see in

[1] So Sanders, *The Codex*, p. 101, and R. R. Johnson, *op. cit.*, pp. 72–3. In the edition
of Persius by Dominicus Bo, Turin, 1969, the editor notes: '"bicolor" autem dicitur
uel quod pars crocea (cf. schol. ad Iuu. vii 23 sq.) pars flaua (cf. Ov. *trist.* iii 1, 3), uel
quod pars candida, pars subnigra erat'.

[2] *Inst. Or.* 3. 31; cf. idem x. 3. 32, where *mutatis codicibus* refers to sets of waxed tablets.
It is an interesting fact that the two earliest *papyrus* note-books that have survived, one
from the third, the other from the fourth century, both leave alternate blank pages as
Quintilian recommended; the former, P. Lit. Lond. 5 + 182, written in a rough hand,
contained Books II–IV of the Iliad and a grammatical text bearing the title Τρύφωνος
τέχνη γραμματική (most recently edited in A. Wouters, *The Grammatical Papyri from
Graeco-Roman Egypt*, no. 2, pp. 61–92); the miscellaneous contents of the latter are
published as P.S.I. i 23 and 34, and viii. 959–60. A parchment notebook of the third
century used for business purposes is illustrated in Plate II. We may also note a *parchment
codex* (if it is a codex) of Homer, of the third(?) century A.D. in which the versos of
the pages are left blank (P. Berol. 10569 = Pack² 689).

[3] The Digest includes quotations from all seven books, cf. Lenel, *Palingenesia*, i, cols.
765–74.

this a very early reference to a codex.[1] But it is much more likely that *membranae* here is a title; *membranae* were so familiar in court that to use it in the title of your work was equivalent to calling it *Jottings from a Lawyer's Notebook*.[2]

As was mentioned at the beginning of this section, all the evidence points to the parchment note-book having been a Roman and not a Greek invention. This is neatly confirmed by the only Greek writer of the first century A.D. to mention the parchment note-book, St Paul. In 2 Timothy iv. 13 he writes: τὸν φαιλόνην ὃν ἀπέλιπον ἐν Τρῳάδι παρὰ Κάρπῳ ἐρχόμενος φέρε, καὶ τὰ βιβλία, μάλιστα τὰς μεμβράνας.[3] The fact that Paul had recourse to a Latin word indicates that he was referring to something which had no recognised Greek designation, and this rules out parchment rolls, for which διφθέραι was readily available. We can thus conclude that Paul's μεμβράναι were of the same nature as the contemporary Roman *membranae*, *i.e.* parchment note-books.

Apart from Paul, the only Greek writer of the first two centuries A.D. to mention the parchment note-book is Galen. In his *De Compositione Medicamentorum* he discusses a preparation alleged to be useful in arresting the spread of baldness and mentions that his friend Claudianus (himself a celebrated doctor) had come across it in a parchment note-book which he had acquired after the owner's death.[4] Why Galen should have recorded the form in which the recipe was found is not clear, unless it was to indicate that it came from a private compilation not intended for publication.

[1] So Schubart, *op. cit.*, pp. 114 sq.

[2] So also Sanders, *The Codex*, p. 103: 'It seems that the title *membranae* recalls the original form and material of the personal note-books which the earlier lawyers used'. Wieacker, *op. cit.*, p. 105 and n. 78 agrees. Dziatzko, *op. cit.*, p. 135, had taken much the same view. An exact parallel to giving his published work a title of this nature is provided by the 'Testament' of Fabricius Veiento, who suffered under Nero, cf. Tacitus, *Ann.*, xiv. 50: *Haud dispari crimine Fabricius Veiento conflictatus est, quod multa et probrosa in patres et sacerdotes composuisset iis libris quibus nomen codicillorum dederat.*

[3] It has been shown (T. C. Skeat, 'Especially the Parchments: a note on 2 Timothy iv. 13', *Journal of Theological Studies* xxx, 1979, pp. 173–7) that μάλιστα here introduces a definition, particularising the general term βιβλία, *i.e.* the μεμβράναι are the βιβλία. It is futile to speculate on the possible contents of these μεμβράναι (ibid., p. 177), nor is the fact that Paul initially describes them as βιβλία significant, since early Christians would not have been concerned with literary or legal distinctions of this kind.

[4] *Opera*, ed. Kuhn, xii. 423: τοῦτο τὸ φάρμακον οὕτω γεγραμμένον εὗρε Κλαυδιανὸς ὁ ἑταῖρος ἡμῶν ἐν πυκτίδι διφθέρᾳ, τοῦ χρωμένου αὐτῷ ἀποθάνοντος. (cf. also iii. 776, where Galen refers to λευκαὶ διφθέραι as bad for the eyes).

It is, however, unnecessary to pursue the parchment note-book further, since already before the end of the first century A.D. a surprising and, as it turned out, decisive step had been taken in the evolution of the codex as a literary form; this will be the subject of the next section.

5

MARTIAL AND THE FIRST APPEARANCE OF
THE CODEX AS A LITERARY FORM

By itself the parchment note-book does not take us very far. In the first two centuries of the Empire polite society acknowledged one form and one form only for the book – the roll. Such was the force of convention that even when the codex was in common use for books Augustine feels obliged to apologize for writing a letter in codex form,[1] and Jerome, who remembers that he is a gentleman as well as a scholar, writes his letters correctly on rolls, even though he keeps his books in codices.[2] The first hint that the dominance of the roll is to be challenged comes towards the end of the first century. We have noticed (p. 18) that Suetonius goes out of his way to mention Julius Caesar's idiosyncratic way of writing his dispatches; and the reason why this impressed him may be found in the works of his contemporary Martial, where we have the first unmistakable reference to literary publication in codex form.[3] The evidence is confined to I. ii – a poem introducing a revised edition of Books I and II reissued together[4] – and to a number of verses in the *Apophoreta*; all alike fall within the years A.D. 84–86.[5] The former runs as follows:

> *Qui tecum cupis esse meos ubicumque libellos*
>   *Et comites longae quaeris habere viae,*
> *Hos eme, quos artat brevibus membrana tabellis:*
>   *Scrinia da magnis, me manus una capit.*
> *Ne tamen ignores ubi sim venalis et erres*
>   *Urbe vagus tota, me duce certus eris:*
> *Libertum docti Lucensis quaere Secundum*
>   *Limina post Pacis Palladiumque forum.*

---

[1] *Ep.* 171.
[2] H. I. Marrou, *Vigiliae Christianae*, iii, 1949, pp. 208 sq.; E. Arns, *La Technique du Livre d'après S. Jérôme*, pp. 120, 122, n. 2.
[3] The word *codex* is never applied by Martial to the books in question.
[4] Or possibly of Books I–VII.
[5] For the chronology of the epigrams see J. W. Duff in *The Oxford Classical Dictionary*, 2nd ed., 1970, (with bibliography); Friedländer, *Sittengeschichte*, iv (Eng. trans.), pp. 36 sq.

The presents for the Saturnalia celebrated in Book XIV, which range from slaves and silver plate to dice and toothpaste, include a number of writing tablets and books. Of the former some are made of ivory or valuable woods, one set is said to be of parchment (*pugillares membranei*). Of the books, some are simply described by their titles – Tibullus, Sallust, the *Thais* of Menander – and are clearly papyrus rolls; others, five in all,[1] have after the name of the author or the work the words *in membranis* or *in pugillaribus membraneis*,[2] the latter expression proving that the books were in codex form and emphasising the small size of those so described. If we read these five epigrams as a group we notice that here again, as in I. 2, Martial is at pains to commend the form of the parchment codex to a public unaccustomed to it, pointing out, for instance how convenient such a book is for the traveller, or how much space it saves in the library when compared with the roll.[3] It has been observed[4] that the authors who appear in this format are all classics and it is likely enough that the fashionable author or discriminating bibliophile would not readily accept a format which suggested the lecture-room or the counting-house; the inference is that these volumes were designed to appeal rather to the literate bourgeoisie.

It has also been questioned whether they were normal books in the sense of complete texts, or whether they were anthologies or extracts of some kind.[5] This doubt is certainly misplaced in the case of the Homer and the Virgil (the epigram on the latter, with its *immensum Maronem*, would lose its point if an anthology were in question), while the Ovid is explicitly stated to contain the entire *Metamorphoses*. The Cicero, it is true, need not have been

[1] *Viz.* 184 (Homer), 186 (Virgil), 188 (Cicero), 190 (Livy), 192 (Ovid, *Metamorphoses*).

[2] On the question whether this should read *membraneis* or *membranis* see Birt, *Buchwesen*, p. 85. F. Bilabel, art. *Membrana* in Pauly-Wissowa, *RE*, points out that Martial's terminology finds a parallel in *CIL* x. 6. 8, an undated inscription mentioning *pugillares membranacei operculis eboreis*; he suggests that it records a gift of books to the Temple of Apollo.

[3] Cf. the discussion in Section 9 of reasons, real or imagined, for the superiority of the codex over the roll.

[4] E.g. by Birt, *Die Buchrolle in der Kunst*, p. 31, and *Abriss*, p. 353.

[5] Cf. F. G. Kenyon, *Books and Readers in Ancient Greece and Rome*, 2nd ed., 1951. He writes (apropos of the epigram on the Livy), p. 94: 'It is evident from this that these were not ordinary copies of the authors named, but were miniatures of some sort, presumably either extracts or epitomes'. Presumably he had in mind the word *artatur* (discussed at length below), though he does not mention it.

more than a selection from the works; but a problem is raised by
the Livy. Do the lines:

> *Pellibus exiguis artatur Livius ingens*
> *Quem mea non totum bibliotheca capit*

really imply that a complete Livy of 142 books had been produced
in codex form?

This has been doubted, both on internal and external grounds.
The internal grounds are founded upon Martial's use of the word
artatur. Originally Birt, in his *Buchwesen* (pp. 85 sq.), regarded
these codices as containing the complete works in each case
(except for the Cicero, where there is nothing in the text of
Martial to oblige us to think that anything more than one or two
works by Cicero were included), but by the time he wrote his
Abriss he regarded them *all* as epitomes or anthologies, in defiance
of the clear meaning of the Latin in at least two instances, namely
Epigram 186 (Virgil) and 192 (Ovid). To justify his view Birt
appealed (p. 349) to the meaning of the word *artare*, which he
claimed implies an epitome or abridgment; but he begs the
question by arguing that when Martial uses the same term for the
collection of his own early epigrams in I. 2 (*hos eme, quos artat*
brevibus membrana tabellis) this re-edition was merely a selection – a
theory for which there is no evidence whatever.

Birt's view can be justified to the extent that *coartare* is used for
abridging a speech for publication as early as Cicero,[1] and
certainly *artare* in later Latin is the technical term for abridgment.
But it can also mean simply 'compressing' or 'confining' (i.e.
between the covers of a book), and when Jerome says '*Esdras et*
Neemias in unum volumen artantur (*Ep.* 53, 8), or mentions '*duodecim*
prophetae in unius voluminis angustias coartati' (*ibid.*)[2] there is clearly
no question of abridgement. But the most powerful refutation of
Birt's views is the argument put forward by, for example,
R. P. Oliver,[3] who points out that if these codices (including the
Livy) 'were extracts or epitomes, the epigrams become pointless,
for there is nothing wonderful about the fact that an epitome is
shorter than the original'.

---

[1] For *coartare = abridge* cf. Cicero, *De Orat*, i, 163, Seneca, *Ep.* 94, 27.

[2] The Twelve (Minor) Prophets contain 3000 στίχοι in the stichometry of Nicephorus,
and could thus have easily been accommodated in a very thin (cf. *angustias*) codex.

[3] *Trans. Am. Phil. Ass.* 82, 1951, pp. 248–9.

It has also been objected that a complete Livy in codex form, which must have filled a large number of volumes, would have been out of scale with other gifts described by Martial, many of which are objects of quite small dimensions. Thus Kenyon (*Books and Readers in Ancient Greece and Rome*[2], p. 94) observes 'A Christmas present of a complete Livy in 142 books is a *reductio ad absurdum*'. But, as has again been pointed out by Oliver[1] 'it would certainly be a fairly expensive gift, but certainly less expensive than such "Christmas presents" as a good cook (xiv. 220), a Spanish girl as accomplished as the one described in 203, or a whole troop of actors (214)'. In short, there are no good reasons for thinking that the Livy was anything other than a complete unabridged text.[2]

One other question which these epigrams raise admits of no answer. The gifts which are the subject of the *Apophoreta* are divided into those intended for the rich and those intended for the poor, and the objects are correspondingly expensive or cheap. The epigrams are arranged in pairs; in each pair, as Martial himself explains (xiv. 1, *Divitis alternas et pauperis accipe sortes*), one epigram describes an expensive present, the other an inexpensive present. But no theory that papyrus books are necessarily dearer than parchment books, or that the reverse is the case,[3] can be maintained without rearranging the order of the epigrams. It is in any case highly probable that the order in this book is disturbed; and it follows that the epigrams cannot be used in the profitless debate (see p. 7 above) on the question whether papyrus or parchment was the more expensive material.

Martial's codices would seem to have been designed for the traveller rather than the bibliophile; reissues of standard authors in pocket format, they were the Elzevirs, if not the Penguins, of their day. They were an innovation; had they not been, there would have been no reason for so emphasizing their superiority to the roll, nor would Martial have gone out of his way in I. 2 to give the address of the publisher where they could be bought. But whether this innovation, marketed jointly by a struggling author and an enterprising publisher, was a success is another question; there are reasons, as we shall see, for thinking that it

[1] Cf. also L. Ascher, 'An Epitome of Livy in Martial's day?', *The Classical Bulletin*, St Louis, 45, 1969, pp. 53–4.

[2] R. R. Johnson, *op. cit.*, pp. 77–8 fully supports Oliver.

[3] The latest proponent of the view that the parchment codices were presents for the rich is R. R. Johnson, *op. cit.*, pp. 78–9.

was not, and in that case it cannot be regarded as the most important link between wooden tablet and modern book. Arguments *ex silentio* are notoriously dangerous, especially in matters of bibliography (it is a sobering thought to consider how different our view of the history of the codex would have been if the poems of Martial had not survived to us), but it is worth noting that in the later years of Martial's literary activity there is no further reference either to the parchment codex or to the publisher Secundus. Nor is there any mention of the parchment codex as a literary form in the writings of other classical authors of the first two centuries, such as the two Plinys, Suetonius, Aulus Gellius, Lucian, Aelius Aristides or Galen, all of whom were bookish men and are well represented by their surviving works; the reference in Galen discussed in p. 22 above certainly relates to the parchment note-book.[1]

Against this silence we can perhaps set the earliest extant fragment of a parchment codex in Latin – the anonymous fragment of a historical work, christened *De bellis Macedonicis*, found at Oxyrhynchus (though not necessarily of Egyptian origin), which has been convincingly attributed, on the ground both of its letter forms and its spelling to a date not far from A.D. 100.[2] But for the moment this fragment stands alone among the remains of Latin literature found in Egypt, the next oldest Latin parchment codex being perhaps the Leiden fragment of the *Sententiae* of Paulus, assigned to the third–fourth century.[3] The most ancient Latin papyrus codices are no older. In any case, the relative scarcity of early Latin fragments from Egypt,[4] coupled with the doubt whether they accurately reflect the reading habits of Rome and the West, warn us against basing any conclusions on such slender evidence.

[1] R. R. Johnson, *op. cit.*, p. 80, n. 1 objects to the inclusion of Greek writers on the ground that they would be less likely to know of a Roman invention. This is true, but overlooks the fact that Lucian worked in Gaul and Italy before settling in Athens, while Galen spent most of the last forty years of his life in Rome. Nor should we forget the Latin literary texts which have come to light in Egypt.

[2] P. Oxy. i 30 = E. A. Lowe, *C.L.A.* ii². 207 and Supplement, p. 47. E. G. Turner, *The Typology of the early Codex*, p. 38, accepts a date early in the second century, but on p. 128, no. 497, it is dated first century.

[3] E. A. Lowe, *C.L.A.*, x. 1577, where the date is given as 'Saec. IV'. Turner, *op. cit.*, p. 126, no. 473 says 'iii–iv'.

[4] The *Corpus Papyrorum Latinarum* of R. Cavenaile, 1958, contains nearly 400 items, as against an estimated 30,000 Greek papyri so far discovered.

To sum up, it appears, so far as we can see, that Martial's experiment was still-born. And if we ask why, an obvious answer lies in the fact that at this time, and throughout the second century, Greek influence in Roman cultural life was perhaps more marked than at any other period; and that in consequence an invention of the practical Latin genius in the field of literature (where convention, we may suspect, governed the form in which a book appeared no less strictly than its composition) would have been at a discount. An additional, or alternative, reason may have been the technical difficulties, discussed in Section 2, of manufacturing parchment on a scale large enough to enable it to provide a viable alternative to papyrus.

Before we leave Martial, there is one final point which deserves consideration. In the poems we have discussed the codex form is so inseparably linked with the use of parchment that scholars have generally regarded it as axiomatic that the parchment codex preceded, and indeed provided the model, for the papyrus codex. To-day this is by no means so certain. The whole matter has been debated at length in Sir Eric Turner's *The Typology of the early Codex*, Chapter 3 (pp. 35–42), 'The Priority of Parchment or Papyrus?', in which he asks the pertinent question: 'If the papyrus codex is confessedly modeled on the parchment codex, why should it at an early date have developed idiosyncratic forms (idiosyncracies which, as a succeeding enquiry will show, may also have extended to its make-up)?'[1] To this question there is as yet no answer; and the possibility cannot be excluded that the papyrus codex, even if it did not antedate the parchment codex, may have developed in parallel with it. At present the question is wide open.

[1] *Op. cit.*, p. 40.

6

THE EVIDENCE OF LEGAL WRITERS

As we have seen, for a century and more after Martial's experiment our literary sources are silent on the development of the codex. The evidence of the classical jurists is thus especially welcome, the more so since they would be expected to take account of general social attitudes rather than reflect the idiosyncracies of individual authors.[1]

Roman lawyers had to decide what the terms 'books' and 'libraries' denoted, particularly when they occurred in wills or bequests. One of the problems they had to face, namely how to distinguish between books and an author's manuscript or notes, does not concern us except insofar as the very existence of the question illustrates how easy it was for a parchment notebook to acquire, almost imperceptibly, the status of a book. But the only question which is relevant to our present enquiry is the following: is the codex a book? Ulpian, writing between A.D. 211 and 217 in connection with bequests, says: '*Librorum appellatione continentur omnia volumina, sive in charta sive in membrana sint sive in quavis alia materia: sed et si in philyra aut in tilia (ut nonnulli conficiunt) aut in quo alio corio, idem erit dicendum. quod si in codicibus sint membraneis vel chartaceis vel etiam eboreis vel alterius materiae vel in ceratis codicillis, an debeantur, videamus. et Gaius Cassius scribit deberi et membranas libris legatis: consequenter igitur cetera quoque debebuntur, si non adversetur voluntas testatoris.*'[2] Then, after discussing the question whether a bequest of *libri* covers unwritten papyrus rolls (*chartae*) and unwritten parchments (*membranae*), he adds: '*Unde non male quaeritur, si libri legati sint, an contineantur nondum perscripti. et non puto contineri, non magis quam vestis appellatione nondum detexta continetur. sed perscripti libri nondum malleati vel ornati continebuntur: proinde et nondum conglutinati*[3] *vel emendati*[4] *continebuntur: sed et membranae nondum consutae continebuntur.*'[5]

---

[1] This point is well made by E. Schönbauer, *IVRA*, 12, 1961, p. 137.

[2] *Digest* xxxii. 52 praef.

[3] On the meaning of these terms cf. Lewis, *Papyrus in Classical Antiquity*, pp. 51–2,

[*Note 3 continued and notes 4 and 5 opposite*

These passages, especially the former, deserve more detailed analysis than they have hitherto received. In the clause *quod si in codicibus sint* etc., the subject of *sint* cannot be, as one might expect, *volumina*, since Ulpian is clearly at pains to draw a distinction between *volumina* and *codices*, and an expression *volumina in codicibus* would thus be a contradiction in terms; it thus seems much more likely that the subject of *sint* is *libri*, understood from the opening words of the passage (*librorum appellatione*). In listing the various forms of writings of which the inclusion in the term *libri* is, for Ulpian, in doubt, he appears to divide them into two classes, the second introduced by the words *vel etiam*, suggesting an even greater degree of dubiety than in the case of those previously mentioned. On this basis the two classes of disputed materials are as follows:

(1)	(2)
codices membranei	*codices eborei*
codices chartacei	*codices alterius materiae*
	cerati codicilli

The question now arises whether the term *codices membranei* denotes, or includes, the parchment notebook which we have already investigated. The repeated association of the parchment notebook with the waxed tablet from which it originated leaves no doubt that Ulpian would have placed it in his Group 2, covered, we may presume, by the words *alterius materiae*. It follows, therefore, that his Group 1 represents papyrus and parchment codices in our sense of the term.

It will be seen that in order to decide whether materials in both these classes are to be accepted as *libri*, Ulpian quotes an opinion of the first century jurisconsult Gaius Cassius which has already been discussed on p. 21 above. It has been objected[1] that the quotation from Cassius does not answer the question posed by Ulpian, but this is to misunderstand Ulpian's reasoning. It is true

---

63, 68–9, especially p. 68: 'It is clear that gluing and malleting were normally thought of not as processes in the manufacture of papyrus sheets but as finishing processes applied to already constructed and even already written rolls'.

[4] *Emendati* perhaps refers to the repair of minor blemishes in the material, cf. Lewis, *op. cit.*, pp. 63–4.

[5] Digest xxxii. 5.

[1] E.g. by Wieacker, *op. cit.*, pp. 105–6. G. G. Archi, *IVRA*, 12, 1961, p. 453 has suggested that the Cassius quotation may be incomplete owing to some words having dropped out in the process of copying, but as shown here this hypothesis is unnecessary.

that Cassius only specifically mentions *membranae*. Given the date at which Cassius was writing this must mean parchment note-books. Ulpian would have argued that since Cassius says *et membranae*, 'even *membranae*' the same must apply (*consequenter*) to all the analogous forms (*cetera*) in his Group 2, and, *a fortiori*, to his Group 1.

It is clear that for Ulpian only the roll was fully and unquestion-ably a 'book'; but it is equally clear that the codex will not long be denied its place. Indeed his contemporary and rival in the law, Paulus, who succeeded him as Praetorian Prefect after his murder in 223, goes further and defines the book is such a way that the codex is at last admitted on terms of equality with the roll (if we may accept the attribution of the *Sententiae*, or at any rate of this quotation, to him): '*Libris legatis tam chartae volumina vel membranae et philyrae continentur: codices quoque debentur: librorum enim appellatione non volumina chartarum, sed scripturae modus qui certo fine concluditur aestimatur*' (iii. 6. 87). The book is now defined, and well defined, as a self-contained unit, independent of material or format. With this judgment the codex has arrived; but it has still to become fashionable. This confirms the verdict of the preceding section, namely that Martial's experiment was not a success, and that the codex emerged as an acceptable form only after a long period of gestation.

The passages from Ulpian and Paulus are both discussed in detail by Wieacker,[1] whose principal hypothesis is that the works of the classical jurists were originally published in roll form; that they were re-copied into codices about A.D. 300; and that hand in hand with this re-copying went an extensive re-editing and alteration of the texts. Wieacker's views, which in any case have been strongly challenged,[2] do not directly concern us except insofar as they involve his contention that the Ulpian and Paulus quotations are not in their original form, but have been largely altered and re-edited. His precise motives in wishing to discredit the evidence of these passages are obscure, but apparently he is concerned that *any* mention of the codex as a possible literary form at this period[3] might imperil his contention that the works of the

[1] *Op. cit.*, pp. 105–6.
[2] E.g. by E. Schönbauer, *IVRA*, 12, 1961, pp. 117–61, and by G. G. Archi, *IVRA*, 12, 1961, pp. 428–50.
[3] It is presumably for this reason that Wieacker makes the fantastic suggestion that it is doubtful whether the well-known fragments of parchment codices with works of

classical jurists were first issued in roll form, and were not transferred to codices until about A.D. 300.

Wieacker's objections to the text of the Ulpian quotation appear to be two: (1) some of the expressions used, such as '*in quavis alia materia*', '*ut nonnulli conficiunt*', '*aut in quo alio corio*', '*vel alterius materiae*', are elaborations which have the odour of the class-room ('Schulstubengeruch'), and (2) as already mentioned, the quotation from Cassius does not really answer the question posed by Ulpian; it is thus presumably, in Wieacker's view, an interpolation, and the consequences drawn from it (*consequenter igitur cetera quoque debebuntur*) must likewise be rejected ('sicher unecht').

There is, of course, no doubt that the final clause of the Ulpian quotation (*si non adversetur voluntas testatoris*), is a later addition, since it runs counter to Ulpian's own line of reasoning, which is a typical interpretation of terms without regard to the probable wishes of the testator. This clause apart, however, Wieacker's arguments are highly subjective, and indeed the only conclusion that even he can draw is that there *may* have been some tampering with the text ('Wir halten eine (vermutlich vorjustinianische) Textveränderung für *möglich*').

In the case of the Paulus quotation, there is general agreement that the *Sententiae* as they have come down to us were put together about A.D. 300, but this does not imply that the individual opinions attributed to Paulus are necessarily unauthentic. Wieacker's sole argument in this instance is that in accepting codices as *libri* the quotation accurately reflects conditions obtaining about A.D. 300, and cannot therefore go back to Paulus himself. It would seem, therefore, that Wieacker rejects the entire passage as unauthentic.

This is, of course something of a *petitio principii*, since Wieacker has to prove not merely that the quotation suits conditions about A.D. 300, but that it does *not* suit conditions in the time of Paulus; and this he has failed to do.

Both Schönbauer[1] and Archi,[2] in addition to their general criticisms of Wieacker's work, have specifically rejected his attacks

Demosthenes and Euripides (below, p. 71) which have been dated to the second century really come from codices ('doch ist nicht erkennbar, ob sie schon Codices sint', *op. cit.*, p. 104, n. 73).

[1] *IVRA*, 12, 1961, pp. 124, 137–8.
[2] Ibid., pp. 434–5.

on the authenticity of the Ulpian and Paulus quotations, and it therefore seems justifiable to continue to use them here as evidence of the increasing prominence of the codex in the Roman world of the early third century.

Before we leave the jurists, there is one more passage from Ulpian which must be briefly mentioned. The text[1] runs: *Si cui centum libri sint legati, centum volumina ei dabimus, non centum, quae quis ingenio suo metitus est, qui ad libri scripturam sufficerent: ut puta cum haberet Homerum totum in uno volumine, non quadraginta octo libros computamus, sed unum Homeri volumen pro libro accipiendum est.* The meaning is perfectly clear, but what is remarkable, and puzzling, is Ulpian's choice of an actual example, namely a complete Homer in one *volumen.* In view of the clear distinction which Ulpian makes between *volumen* and *codex, volumen* here can only mean a (papyrus) roll. But it is unnecessary to demonstrate that a complete Homer in a single roll is a physical impossibility; and since tens of thousands of Homeric manuscripts must have been in existence at the time, this impossibility would have been immediately obvious to Ulpian's readers. We must therefore conclude that the example was a purely hypothetical or imaginary one.

To the papyrologist of to-day, of course, the impossibility of the example is equally obvious. But it might not have been so had we no Homeric fragments from Egypt to help us. If nothing else, this passage shows how careful we must be in taking what appears to be factual evidence at its face value.

[1] *Digest* xxxii 52 § 1.

7

ROLL AND CODEX: EVIDENCE OF GREEK LITERARY TEXTS OF THE FIRST FIVE CENTURIES

In the preceding sections the literary evidence for the emergence of the codex form has been examined. We now turn to the evidence of the actual manuscripts which have survived from this period. But before we do so, a few words of caution must be given. An overwhelming proportion of these manuscripts come from Egypt, and because of the chance nature of discoveries we cannot be certain either that they are typical of Egypt as a whole, or, if this is conceded, that what was typical of Egypt was necessarily typical of the Graeco-Roman world as a whole.

The former of these points can be the more readily answered. Apart from the Delta and Alexandria, discoveries have been made in almost every region of Egypt, and serious though the absence of Alexandria is, it is probable that many of the literary papyri found at Oxyrhynchus, where wealthy Alexandrians possessed country estates, either were written in Alexandria, or, if local copies, would have reflected current fashions in the capital.[1]

The second question is much less easy to answer. However, the ease of travel throughout the Roman world, the continual movements of officials, merchants and others, and, above all, the unchallenged reputation of Alexandria in matters of bibliography, all suggest that there is unlikely to have been any great differences in the construction of books between Egypt and the rest of the Empire.

There are indeed other and more serious reservations to be made in the assessment of the Egyptian evidence. The dating of literary papyri is far from being an exact science, and estimates of date may vary by a century or more. All we can hope for is that the inevitable errors in dating will, at least to some extent,

[1] For the criteria by which we may hope to distinguish papyri of Alexandrian origin (whether immediately or ultimately) cf. E. G. Turner, *Greek Papyri*, pp. 92–5.

cancel each other out. A further difficulty is the distribution in time. Relatively abundant during the first three centuries, the output of literary papyri shows a dramatic falling-off after A.D. 300 which presumably reflects the general decay of Hellenism.[1] However, we can only take the evidence as we find it.

The statistics which follow are based on the data in Pack[2] (1965), supplemented by (a) F. Uebel, *Literarische Texte unter Ausschluss der Christlichen* in *Archiv für Papyrusforschung*, 21, 1971, pp. 170–182, for publications up to about 1970, and (b) the section *Testi recentemente pubblicati: Testi letterari greci* in *Aegyptus*, 51, 1971, pp. 227–30; 52, 1972, pp. 163–8; 53, 1973, pp. 160–4; 54, 1974, pp. 206–9; 55, 1975, pp. 275–9; 57, 1977, pp. 202–47; 58, 1978, 225–87; and 60, 1980, pp. 233–65. In the case of papyrus and parchment codices much use has been made of E. G. Turner, *The Typology of the early Codex*, 1977, which covers (see p. xxii) material published up to November 1973. It should be made clear that except in a few cases the figures are based on the estimates of date given by the original editors. The employment of dates spanning two centuries, e.g., second–third century, has a certain disadvantage in that it gives the impression that there was a diminution of literary activity during each of these bridging periods. This was not, of course, the case but merely reflects the predilection of editors for assigning a text to a particular century. There is indeed a method whereby this disadvantage can be eliminated. William H. Willis in *A census of the Literary Papyri from Egypt* (*Greek, Roman and Byzantine Studies*, 9, 1968, pp. 205–41) divides the texts spanning two centuries equally between the centuries concerned, presumably on the grounds that of all the texts dated by their editors, e.g., second–third century, there is a statistical probability that in fact 50% will have been written in the second century and 50% in the third. This expedient has not been adopted here, since it involves a re-interpretation of the judgments of the original editors. Fortunately the principal points which emerge from the survey remain substantially the same whichever procedure is followed.

The figures below cover all Greek (but not Latin) literary and scientific writings, Christian literature excepted; they omit items

---

[1] There may be other factors; for instance, the well-known scarcity of dated documents of the fifth century A.D. may be paralleled by a corresponding dearth of literary texts from the same period.

which are, or appear to be, school exercises, single sheets, mathematical tables – anything in short which is clearly not a book. For the same reason items such as waxed or wooden tablets, ostraca, and inscriptions on stone or metal are of course excluded. It should be added that since we are here concerned with format, *i.e.* whether a manuscript is in roll or codex form, no distinction is made between texts on papyrus and those on parchment. The unit in these statistics is the book, *i.e.* where a single roll or codex comprises two or more different works it is counted as only one unit. However, where a roll has been re-used by having a different literary work written on the verso, the texts on recto and verso are each counted as one unit, since the scribe of the verso text was presumably satisfied with the roll format and only used a discarded roll instead of a new one for reasons of economy.

Century	Rolls	Codices	Total	% Rolls*	% Codices*
I	252	1	253	100	0
I–II	203	4	207	98	2
II	857	14	871	$98\frac{1}{2}$	$1\frac{1}{2}$
II–III	349	17	366	$95\frac{1}{2}$	$4\frac{1}{2}$
III	406	93	499	$81\frac{1}{2}$	$18\frac{1}{2}$
III–IV	54	50	104	52	48
IV	36	99	135	$26\frac{1}{2}$	$73\frac{1}{2}$
IV–V	7	68	75	$9\frac{1}{2}$	$90\frac{1}{2}$
V	11	88	99	11	89

* To nearest $\frac{1}{2}$%

From these figures it is clear that the codex scarcely counted for Greek literature before about A.D. 200. Nevertheless its representation is not, as has sometimes been suggested, entirely negligible. The significance of these second-century codices for the origins and growth of the codex form in non-Christian literature will be discussed in Section 12. For the present, however, the fact remains that it was only in the course of the third century that the codex obtained a significant share of book-production and it was not until about A.D. 300 that it achieved parity with the roll.

8

THE CODEX IN EARLY CHRISTIAN LITERATURE

As we have seen, in the pagan world of the second century the codex has barely a foothold. In the contemporary Christian world the position is very different, and it is to this that we must look for the origins of the modern book. The assembling of statistics in the field of Christian papyri has been immeasurably lightened by two recent publications, *viz.* Kurt Aland, *Repertorium der griechischen Christlichen Papyri*: I, *Biblische Papyri*, 1976, and Joseph van Haelst, *Catalogue des Papyrus littéraires juifs et chrétiens*, 1976, the second being of especial value for the present investigation since it includes for the first time a survey of all Christian papyri, both Biblical and non-Biblical. The data from these two publications have been supplemented by the bibliographies of Kurt Treu, *Christliche Papyri* VI and VII, in *Archiv für Papyrusforschung* 26, 1978, pp. 149–59, and 27, 1980, pp. 251–8 respectively. It should be noted that whereas Aland's work is strictly limited to texts on papyrus, the publication of van Haelst, despite its title, includes texts on all kinds of material, as also do the bibliographies of Treu.

On the basis of the information furnished by the foregoing publications it can be calculated that there are approximately 172 Biblical manuscripts or fragments of manuscripts written before A.D. 400 or not long thereafter (*i.e.* including items which have been dated fourth–fifth century). This number leaves out of account Biblical papyri of the Ptolemaic period, which must necessarily be of Jewish origin, and all manuscripts on materials other than papyrus or parchment, together with items such as amulets, school- or writing-exercises, single sheets, etc., – everything in fact which is clearly not a book. Of these 172 items, 98 come from the Old Testament and 74 from the New. So far as we can judge – and in some cases decision is difficult for various reasons[1] – 158 texts come from codices and only 14 from rolls. A

---

[1] E.g., in the case of a small fragment written on both sides, the difficulty of distinguishing between a codex and an opisthograph roll, cf. E. G. Turner, *The Typology of the early codex*, pp. 9–10.

closer examination makes the disparity even sharper. For this purpose it is desirable to list the 14 rolls, adding the numbers in the Catalogue of Van Haelst:

1 P. Oxy. ix. 1166. Genesis. Van Haelst 14.
2 P. Oxy. viii. 1075. Exodus (recto), Apocalypse (verso). Van Haelst 44, 559.
3 P. Oxy. x. 1225. Leviticus. Van Haelst 48.
4 Stud. Pal. xv. 234. Psalms. Van Haelst 104.
5 P. Lit. Lond. 207. Psalms. Van Haelst 109.
6 P. Lips. Inv. 39. Psalms. Van Haelst 133.
7 P. Harr. 31. Psalms. Van Haelst 148.
8 Stud. Pal. xi. 114. Psalms. Van Haelst 167.
9 P.S.I. viii. 921. Psalms. Van Haelst 174.
10 P. Lond. Inv. 2584. Hosea-Amos. Van Haelst 286.
11 P. Alex. Inv. 203. Isaiah. Van Haelst 300.
12 P. Lit. Lond. 211. Daniel. Van Haelst 319.
13 P. Oxy. x. 1228. John. Van Haelst 459.
14 P. Oxy. iv. 657 + P.S.I. xii. 1292. Hebrews. Van Haelst 537.

Of these 14, five (nos. 5, 6, 9, 10, 14) are opisthograph, *i.e.* the Biblical text is written on the back of a re-used roll, which thus imposed the roll format. This reduces the number of 'genuine' rolls to nine. Of these nine, three (nos. 7, 8, 12) are probably of Jewish origin,[1] and two more (nos. 1 and 3) possibly so.[2] This leaves only nos. 2, 4, 11 and 13 to be considered. The last-named is an eccentric production, being written on the verso of a roll the recto of which is left blank. Various complicated explanations of this phenomenon have been proposed,[3] but for the present purpose we can reasonably leave it out of account. No. 2 is opisthograph, but has Biblical texts on both sides. The Exodus is presumably Christian, since κύριος is abbreviated (although υἱός and Ἰσραήλ are not). Nevertheless, from any point of view the item is clearly an oddity, and we are thus left with only two normal rolls of Christian origin, *viz.* nos. 4 and 11. As regards no. 4, the Psalms were used for such a variety of purposes, devotional,

[1] On the criteria for deciding whether manuscripts of the Greek Old Testament are of Christian or Jewish origin see C. H. Roberts, *Manuscript, Society and Belief in early Christian Egypt*, pp. 74–8. The three papyri here mentioned are discussed on p. 77.
[2] Ibid., where no. 1 is described as 'perhaps more likely to be Christian than Jewish' and no. 3 is classed among the *dubia*.
[3] Cf. K. Aland, *Studien zur Überlieferung des Neuen Testaments und seines Textes*, p. 114.

liturgical, magical, etc., that this exception has less significance. The Isaiah has the *nomen sacrum* for κύριος, and is therefore presumably Christian and a genuine exception.[1] It may be added that no text of any part of the New Testament is known written on the recto of a roll.

If we examine these 172 Biblical manuscripts from a different standpoint, we find that there are eleven which in our opinion may be assigned to the second century and are thus the earliest Christian manuscripts in existence. All are on papyrus and in codex form. The following list[2] includes references to the work of van Haelst, and we have also, because of the particular importance of dating, appended references to E. G. Turner, *The Typology of the early codex*,[3] in which he records both his own judgments and those of other scholars.

1 P. Ryl. iii. 457. John. Van Haelst 462. *Typology* P 52. ii.
2 P. Baden iv. 56. Exodus, Deuteronomy. Van Haelst 33. *Typology* OT 24. (ii ed.; late ii E.G.T.).
3 P. Yale i. 1. Genesis. Van Haelst 12. *Typology* OT 7. ii/iii (E.G.T.; A.D. 90 ed.).
4 P. Chester Beatty VI. Numbers, Deuteronomy.[4] Van Haelst 52. *Typology* OT 36. ii/iii (E.G.T., A. S. Hunt; ii F. G. Kenyon, U. Wilcken).
5 P. Ant. i. 7. Psalms. Van Haelst 179. *Typology* OT 120. ii/iii (E.G.T.; ed., ii H.I.Bell).
6 P. Lips. Inv. 170. Psalms. Van Haelst 224. *Typology* OT 151. iii (ii C.H.R.).
7 Oxford, Bodleian MS. Gr. bibl. g. 5 (P) Psalms. Van Haelst 151. *Typology* OT 97 A. ii/iii (E.G.T.; ii ed.).
8 P. Barc. Inv. 1 + Magdalen College, Oxford, Gr. 18 + Paris, Bibliothèque nationale, Suppl. Gr. 1120. Matthew, Luke.

---

[1] Cf. C. H. Roberts, *op. cit.*, p. 31, n. 1: 'What is true is that the contracted form of κύριος is in the first three centuries the mark of a Christian manuscript'. Van Haelst's verdict of 'probablement juif' is presumably based on the fact that it is a roll.

[2] The list is identical with that in C. H. Roberts, *op. cit.*, pp. 13–14, which gives a little more detail about one or two of the texts.

[3] The references are to the identification numbers of the manuscripts in the 'Consolidated List of codices consulted' at the end of the book.

[4] On the date of this manuscript, which occupies a key position among early Christian texts, see Roberts, *op. cit.*, Appendix II, pp. 78–81, where the conclusion is reached (p. 81) that 'on present evidence a second century date, though possible or even probable, is not necessary and a provisional verdict should be second/third century'.

Van Haelst 336, 403. *Typology* P 4, P 64, P 67. iii or iii/iv (P 4), ii (P 64, 67).

9 P. Ryl. i. 5. Titus. Van Haelst 534. *Typology* P 32. iii (ii Bell-Skeat).

10 P. Oxy. xxxiv. 2683. Matthew. Van Haelst 372. *Typology* P 77. ii.

11 P. Oxy. 50. 3523. John. ii. Not in *Typology*.

We have excluded from the list a second-century codex of Genesis,[1] since in spite of the codex form we consider it to be of Jewish origin. The above eleven are without exception Christian. To these may be added four other Christian non-Biblical texts which in our opinion are to be assigned to the second century:

12 British Library Egerton Papyrus 2. Unknown Gospel. Van Haelst 586. *Typology* NT Apocrypha 7. ii.

13 P. Mich. 130. Hermas, *Shepherd*. Van Haelst 657. Not in *Typology* (written on verso of a roll).

14 P. Oxy. i. 1. Gospel of Thomas. Van Haelst 594. *Typology* NT Apocrypha 1. ii/iii.

15 P. Oxy. iii. 405. Irenaeus, *Adversus Haereses*. Van Haelst 671. Not in *Typology* (a roll).

It should be emphasised that, as will have been evident from the *Typology* references, not all scholars agree about the dates to be assigned to these fourteen manuscripts. Some would find our list too inclusive,[2] others too restricted;[3] but about some in the above lists (nos. 1, 2, 8, 10, 12) there is unanimity.[4]

As already stated, all the above Biblical manuscripts (nos. 1–11) are codices, while of the other four (nos. 12–15) the only true exception is the roll of Irenaeus (no. 15), since the Hermas (no. 13) is written on the verso of a roll carrying a documentary text and the scribe thus had no option in his choice of format. The

---

[1] P. Oxy. iv. 656. Van Haelst 13. *Typology* OT 9. ii/iii (E.G.T.; iii ed.; ii Bell/Skeat).

[2] Cf. E. G. Turner, *Typology*, p. 4 and, for Turner's own list of second century Christian codices, p. 90, nos. p C 201–5.

[3] Conspicuous among manuscripts which some scholars have placed in the second century are: the Bodmer St John (P. Bodmer II; van Haelst 426; *Typology* P 66. iii); the Chester Beatty Papyrus IX, Ezekiel, Daniel, Esther; (van Haelst 315; *Typology* OT 183.iii E.G.T.; Wilcken, Galiano ii); and Chester Beatty Papyrus VIII, Jeremiah (van Haelst 304; *Typology* OT 202 iv E.G.T.; ii or ii/iii Kenyon).

[4] On factors influencing the dating of early Christian papyri see Roberts, *op. cit.*, p. 12, n. 2.

distinction between Biblical and non-Biblical texts would not have been so obvious to the users of these as it is to us, and both the Egerton Gospel and the *Shepherd* of Hermas might have been regarded as indistinguishable from the canonical books of the New Testament. Even if we give this extended meaning to the term 'Biblical', the conclusion remains the same, namely that when the Christian Bible first emerges into history the books of which it was composed are always written on papyrus and are always in codex form. There could not be a greater contrast in format with the non-Christian book of the second century, a contrast all the more remarkable when we recall that Egypt, where all these early Christian texts were found, was the country where the papyrus roll originated and where the status of the roll as the only acceptable format for literature was guaranteed by Alexandria with its dominating position in the world of books.[1]

The question may be raised whether the contrast between the Christian and non-Christian book is equally marked in the case of non-Biblical literature. As we have just observed, the distinction between Biblical and non-Biblical works is, at any rate in the second century, to some extent anachronistic: however, for the vast majority of the works we have now to consider there was never any question of their being given canonical status or of their enjoying an authoritative position in the period before the emergence of the Canon. The range of these writings is very wide, and in analysing them we have followed the divisions of van Haelst's Catalogue into Apocrypha, Patristica, Liturgica, Hagiographica and Miscellaneous (this last section includes anonymous homilies and treatises and not a few texts whose character is quite uncertain). The chronological period covered here is the same as that for Biblical texts; and we have used the same sources (p. 38),

---

[1] Of course, the fact that all known specimens of early Christian papyri come from Egypt is fortuitous and does not prove that the codex originated there (the fragment of Tatian's *Diatessaron* found at Dura on the Euphrates is part of a parchment roll). On the question whether the papyrus codex was of Egyptian origin E. G. Turner writes (*Typology* p. 40): 'There can be no automatic presumption that the codex of papyrus is restricted to Egypt'. And if Christians are to be credited with the invention of the papyrus codex, Egypt, for the reasons given above, is less likely to have been the country of its invention than, e.g. Syria. But wherever the papyrus codex originated, we have still to explain how it managed to establish itself in Egypt in face of the total domination of the roll: as Turner puts it (*ibid.*) 'In Egyptian book technique the papyrus roll was so firmly entrenched that a major shock was needed to prompt the experiments that resulted in its eventually being supplanted by the codex'.

and have again included only what can properly be regarded as books or fragments of books. We have applied the term Christian strictly: works with Christian references, e.g., the Sibylline Oracles and works of magic, as well as Jewish texts, have been excluded, although there are some cases in which the decision between Jewish and Christian is difficult to make. The analysis is one of works, not of manuscripts; since one of our objects is to discover the kind of work for which either a roll or a codex was chosen, a codex will be counted more than once if it includes, as some do, several different texts.

Within these limits are found 118 texts, 14 of which are written on parchment and 104 on papyrus. For 83 of these the codex form was chosen. The remaining 35 are rolls, 3 of them opisthograph. By themselves these figures are not particularly instructive; we have to consider not so much the date of writing as the category of the work. Given that there is no example of any of the four Canonical Gospels being written on the recto of a roll (*i.e.* in roll form by choice) we might expect that any other Gospel which resembled them in narrating the life or recording the teaching of Jesus (e.g., the Egerton Gospel) would circulate in the same format; this would not necessarily apply to such works as those of the Gnostic Gospels which are in fact theological treatises, or the Infancy Gospels. Such a differentiation would be all the more likely if the Christian adoption of the codex originated, as suggested below (p. 59), in the use of tablets for recording the Oral Law. Similarly, whereas we have seen that the codex form was closely associated in the second and third centuries with the books essential for the Christian mission, *viz.* the books of the Old Testament together with such Christian works as were deemed authoritative, we might not expect to find the codex so widely used for works of general Christian literature: a theological treatise such as that of Irenaeus already noticed (p. 41) might well have been expected to adopt the form conventional for academic works. The picture, however, is not quite so clear-cut as this.

The first of the categories into which the 118 texts divide is that of Apocrypha. Among the very varied works ranged under this heading there are 10 possible examples of Gospels as we have defined them. Both the second century examples are codices, as we have noted above (nos. 12 and 14). Of the remaining 8, both manuscripts of the Gospel of Thomas are rolls; so too is the so-called Fayum Gospel and an Oxyrhynchus fragment dated to about A.D. 200 and now plausibly assigned to the banned Gospel of Peter,[1] while a roll is also the format of the only surviving manuscript of the Greek Diatessaron, if that work may be fairly classified here. The remaining 3 manuscripts are codices. The other apocryphal texts, 23 in number, and including Infancy Gospels and Acts of various Apostles, are exclusively codices.

In the Patristic section of 39 texts, two works, the Epistle of Barnabas and the *Shepherd* of Hermas, both of which had some claim to canonical status, are represented, the former by 2 codices, the latter by 2 rolls (one of which is opisthograph) and 9 codices.[2] Of the remaining 26 texts 6, including 3 manuscripts of Irenaeus, are rolls and 20 are codices.

In view of the persistent use of the roll in the liturgy of the Eastern Church (see below, p. 51, n. 6) it is not surprising that 6 of the 11 texts in the Liturgical section are on rolls.

The single hagiographical text which falls within our period is a codex. In the miscellaneous section we have 16 rolls and 21 codices; the rolls (if we ignore 2 the nature of which is quite uncertain) are all treatises or homilies (only one is opisthograph), and their significant proportion testifies to the maintenance of the literary tradition.

To sum up, although the majority of Christian non-Biblical texts are in codex form, an appreciable minority are on rolls, and this minority approaches significance in precisely those categories where we should expect to find it. At the same time the contrast with secular literature, though not quite so marked as in the case of Biblical texts, is nevertheless still striking.

We have now to consider possible reasons for this remarkable predilection of the early Christians for the codex form, and endeavour to formulate hypotheses which would at the same time explain the divergence of treatment accorded to Biblical and non-Biblical texts.

[1] See D. Lührmann in *ZNTW*, 72, 1981, pp. 216–26.
[2] Two further papyri of this work, both of the third century and both codices, will be published in P. Oxy. 50.

9

WHY DID CHRISTIANS ADOPT THE CODEX? INADEQUACY OF PRACTICAL CONSIDERATIONS

THE reasons adduced by Martial[1] in favour of the parchment codex, even if Secundus's experiment had not been the failure it pretty certainly was, are quite inadequate to explain what was not merely a preference by the Christian communities for the codex form, but an exclusive devotion to it, and that too not only for the books of the New Testament but for those of the Old Testament as well, and from the earliest period for which evidence has survived. Indeed so universal is the Christian use of the codex in the second century that its introduction must date well before A.D. 100. It is, moreover, significant for the history of the early Church that Christian book-production methods should have severed themselves from Jewish so completely and at so early a date: that the Christians transcribed the books of the Septuagint onto codices illustrates how complete the severance was.

It has been widely assumed that the codex must have possessed some significant practical advantages over the roll. A variety of such explanations have been put forward, and it will be convenient to discuss them in detail at this point. Before doing so, however, one thing must be made clear, namely that there are two quite separate problems, firstly why Christians adopted the codex for their writings from the outset, and secondly why (though only over a period of several centuries) the codex eventually displaced the roll in the field of non-Christian literature as well. The practical reasons which we shall consider here will not necessarily have the same force for both these processes, and this is a factor which must be borne in mind.

1. *Economy.* This is the reason most commonly put forward, and one of the most obvious and apparently convincing. Since the codex makes use of both sides of the writing material instead of

---

[1] See Section 5 above.

only one, the cost of producing a manuscript would be reduced. There was, of course, no reason why the verso of a roll should not be used for a continuation of the work on the recto, but the very small number of such rolls (the roll in Apocalypse v. 1, γεγραμμένον ἔσωθεν καὶ ὄπισθεν, is perhaps the best known example) shows that this was not regarded as a satisfactory method. But how much would the saving by using the codex format amount to? It is unlikely that the cost would be halved, since the expense of writing would be the same in either case, at least if the manuscripts were professionally written. The Christian manuscripts of the second century, although not reaching a high standard of calligraphy, generally exhibit a competent style of writing which has been called 'reformed documentary'[1] and which is likely to be the work of experienced scribes, whether Christian or not; certainly there is nothing in the nature of privately made copies such as the celebrated manuscript of Aristotle's Constitution of Athens.[2] And it is therefore a reasonable assumption that the scribes of the Christian texts received pay for their work. Nothing is known of the general level of book-prices in antiquity, but some very rough calculations suggest that by employing the codex format the cost of producing a book might be reduced by about one quarter.[3] In a specific instance, the early third century manuscript of the Pauline Epistles in the Chester Beatty collection might have cost about 28 drachmae if written in roll form, and about $20\frac{1}{2}$ drachmae if written in a codex – a saving of $7\frac{1}{2}$ drachmae. The Pauline Epistles in the Beatty codex are about twice as long as an average Gospel, the saving on which would thus be only half this amount.

It seems very unlikely that this reduction in cost would have been sufficient to account for the fundamental change from the roll to the codex. In fact, if economy was such a decisive factor, one would expect to find some traces of other attempts to make the most economical use of the writing material; but such traces are conspicuous by their absence. Scripts are of a normal size, and are not noticeably small or compressed, although had they wished

---

[1] Roberts, *op. cit.*, pp. 14–15.

[2] One possible exception is P. Baden 4. 56, of which Aland says 'es handelt sich sehr wahrscheinlich um eine private Abschrift'.

[3] T. C. Skeat, 'The length of the standard papyrus roll and the cost-advantage of the codex', *Zeitschrift für Papyrologie und Epigraphik*, 45, 1982, pp. 169–75.

to do so there would have been nothing to stop Christian scribes from adopting a script as small as that of the second century codex of the Republic of Plato discussed below (**P. Oxy. xliv. 3157**). No attempt is made to reduce the margins surrounding the written area: on the contrary, in what may be one of the earliest of the second century Christian codices, the Chester Beatty Numbers and Deuteronomy, the margins at the top and bottom of the page are exceptionally large, the upper margin having been originally about $2\frac{1}{2}$ ins. = 6.35 cm and the lower margin 3 ins. = 7.62 cm. Finally, although as we have seen there are a few examples of Christian books written on the backs of re-used rolls, these are not (except for the Psalms fragment, no. 9 in the list on p. 39) especially early. There is no evidence at all for the employment of palimpsests, *i.e.* papyri from which the original writing had been washed off to enable them to be re-used. All-in-all, the argument from economy would seem to be negligible.

2. *Compactness.* This is a serious and valid argument, since it is mentioned by Martial as one of the advantages of the codex, particularly for reading on a journey. That the codex is more compact than the roll is undeniable, since the actual volume of papyrus used is reduced by almost one-half. The codex could also be more easily and economically stacked and shelved, though this is an argument more likely to appeal to owners of libraries than to the early Christian communities. And while a codex is obviously more compact and convenient than an assemblage of rolls, at the time when the Christians are presumed to have adopted the codex, *viz.* not later than A.D. 100, it is probable that Gospels were still circulating singly, and the virtue of compactness would have been much less evident. In fact, a roll 18 cm high and 6 m in length could be rolled into a cylinder 3 or 4 cm in diameter, which could be comfortably held between thumb and forefinger. Such a roll could easily have accommodated any one of the canonical Gospels or the Acts of the Apostles if written in the same style as P⁴ (no. 8 in the list on p. 40). A codex of the same capacity would measure about 18 × 14 cm by about 1 cm thick, exclusive of any binding. But manuscripts of the Septuagint would also have been required, and here the superiority of the codex is more easily demonstrable. If we take as an example the Chester Beatty codex of Numbers and Deuteronomy (no. 4 in the list) it can be calculated that if written in the same style in the form of a roll,

it would have needed about 28 m of papyrus[1] – a very bulky roll indeed, and far beyond the limit of convenient handling. A codex the size of the Numbers and Deuteronomy manuscript could have contained the entire Psalter, an obvious advantage since the Pentateuch and the Psalter provided the bulk of the Old Testament passages exploited by the early Christians. It could also have accommodated the whole of Marcion's 'New Testament', consisting of a 'purified' text of Luke and ten Pauline Epistles.

Nevertheless it seems to have taken several centuries for the full potential of the codex to be recognised. Up to the third century no surviving codex is known to have had more than 150 leaves = 300 pages,[2] and many are much smaller. But thereafter they grow to much greater proportions. One of the Coptic Manichaean codices (the Psalm-Book, fourth–fifth cent.) had at least 638 pages,[3] while the great parchment codices of the entire Bible, the Codex Vaticanus and the Codex Sinaiticus (fourth cent.) contained at least 1600 and 1460 pages respectively, while the Codex Alexandrinus (fifth cent.) had at least 1640. By now the advantage of the codex was evident to all, and not merely for Christian literature; thus, the first 35 rolls of Ulpian's *Ad Edictum* were republished in three codices containing the text of 14, 11 and 7 rolls respectively,[4] while Gregory the Great remarks that within the compass of 6 codices he has compressed a work which had occupied 35 rolls.[5]

To sum up, compactness was clearly an important factor in the early Christians' choice of the codex: the only doubt is whether it was so fully appreciated at the time when the decision was made.

3. *Comprehensiveness.* This is virtually another facet of the argument from compactness just discussed. Comprehensiveness is here taken to mean the ability to bring together within two covers texts which had hitherto circulated separately. A comprehensive codex might consist either of a single literary work extending over a number of rolls; a 'collected edition' or a representative selection of works by a single author or on a single theme; or quite

---

[1] The calculation is as follows: the Beatty codex originally consisted of 216 pages, each of 2 columns = 432 columns, the average width of which is 5 cm. The intercolumniations are about 1.5 cm wide, and 432 × 6.5 cm = 2808 cm = 28 m.

[2] The largest so far known is the Philo codex from Oxyrhynchus, which had at least 289 pages, cf. Turner, *Typology*, p. 82.

[3] Ibid.   [4] F. Wieacker, *Textstufen klassischer Juristen*, pp. 127–8.

[5] Ep. 5, 53a.

simply a miscellany; and examples of all these are found. The earliest and most striking examples of comprehensive codices are Greek Biblical manuscripts, beginning with the Chester Beatty codices of Gospels and Acts and the Pauline Epistles and leading on to the complete Bibles of the fourth and fifth centuries mentioned above. Another form of the comprehensive codex was created by binding up together a number of smaller codices, a common practice in the Middle Ages. The changes of hand, discontinuous pagination, and differences in the sizes of quires suggest that the Bodmer 'composite' codex, analysed in E. G. Turner, *The Typology of the early codex*, pp. 79–80, may be of this type. Alternatively, a single scribe may copy out a variety of heterogeneous texts, and examples of this are listed by Turner, *op. cit.*, pp. 81–2.

As regards the question whether the quality of comprehensiveness may have influenced the early Christians in their choice of the codex, the answer must be much the same as in the case of compactness, namely that it is doubtful whether it can have been an important factor as early as A.D. 100.

4. *Convenience of use.* It has been claimed that the codex is more convenient to handle than the roll, because two hands are needed to hold the manuscript, one to unwind a convenient length for reading, the other to roll up the already read portion. This is true, but the codex equally required two hands, one to hold the volume, the other to turn the pages, unless the book is rested on a desk or table. As regards the supposed awkwardness of unrolling the roll in the process of reading, it is probable that practice made this an automatic action performed with no more conscious effort than turning the pages of a book.

Re-rolling the roll after it has been read through to the end, a necessary proceeding to enable the next reader to start at the beginning, is another reason which has been put forward in favour of the codex, and this certainly has some validity. However, practical experiments have shown[1] that the supposed difficulty and time-consuming nature of the task have been greatly exaggerated, and this is hardly a factor likely to have influenced the early Christians, any more than it influenced the Jews either then or later. Certainly no ancient writer is known to have alluded to

[1] Cf. T. C. Skeat, 'Two notes on Papyrus: 1. Was re-rolling a papyrus roll an irksome and time-consuming task?', *Scritti in onore di Orsolina Montevecchi*, 1981, pp. 373–6.

the problem which, one suspects, is based on nothing more than a projection back into the past of the probable reactions of a present-day reader.

5. *Ease of reference*. It has been suggested that it would have been much easier to locate a particular passage in a Biblical text written in codex form than it would be in a roll, and that this would have been a decided advantage in the cut and thrust of theological debate. Since a codex could be opened at a particular place much more quickly than a roll could be unrolled to find the same passage, this certainly appears to be a strong argument: one thinks of Augustine in the famous 'Tolle, lege' episode, when he kept a finger in the codex of the Pauline Epistles to mark the place of the providential passage he had found. But it must be remembered that in the ancient world there was no such thing as exact quotation in the sense of giving the precise location of a particular passage. The only available means of so doing was by means of stichometry, and there are in fact a very few examples, both Greek and Latin,[1] of the position of a passage being indicated either by stating by how many *stichoi* it came from the beginning of the work, or, more rarely, from the end. This would, of course, give only an approximate idea of where to look for the passage, unless the reader was prepared to count the text in *stichoi* himself. For more immediate and accurate location the text would have to be equipped with marginal stichometry, e.g. for every hundred *stichoi* to be noted in the margin, and this is far from common. And of course if the manuscript was so equipped the passage could be located irrespective of whether the manuscript was a roll or a codex.[2] How little use was made of stichometry as a means of reference is illustrated by the fact that in manuscripts of poetry or drama, where line-numeration could very easily have been introduced, this seemingly obvious step was never taken.[3]

It has also been suggested that page-numeration, which is a

---

[1] K. Ohly, *Stichometrische Untersuchungen*, 1928, pp. 109–18.

[2] H. Ibscher, in *Jahrbuch der Einbandkunst*, 4, 1937, p. 4, actually claimed that for the purpose of reference the roll was just as convenient as the codex ('Selbst als Nachschlagewerk eignete sich die Buchrolle genau so gut wie der Codex').

[3] Although there are some examples of verse and drama texts with stichometric marks every hundred lines, these clearly would have been of little use for reference. To be of practical use, it would have been necessary to mark the text at much more frequent intervals, say every five lines, as in modern editions. The absence of any such system proves that the stichometric markings just mentioned could not provide, and were not intended to provide, a means of reference.

feature of many early Christian codices[1] (the earliest are perhaps the Chester Beatty Numbers and Deuteronomy and the Egerton Gospel), was devised to facilitate reference. But in the whole of ancient literature there is no example of a page-reference being given, and the reason is obvious, namely that no two manuscripts are identical and pagination will thus be different in every case.[2] Moreover, had this been the intention the pagination would have been inserted at the outset, whereas in fact it has often been added by a later hand or hands. It is much more likely that pagination, which in any case is not invariable, was merely a device for keeping the pages in the right order during the process of binding and – perhaps even more important – to ensure that none were missing. All this is confirmed by the fact that in later centuries[3] pagination is replaced by quire numeration, which fulfils the same function.

6. *The medieval experience.* Overshadowing all the practical arguments in favour of the codex discussed above is the massive use made of rolls throughout the Middle Ages and even later.[4] Although for literature of all kinds the codex reigns supreme, for administrative records the roll long continues to be the dominant format.[5] This is particularly the case in England, where many great series of state records were kept in roll form for upwards of six centuries, some, like the Patent Rolls, literally down to the present day.[6]

[1] On the pagination of early codices see E. G. Turner, *Typology*, pp. 75–7.

[2] Compilers of medieval library lists capitalised on this by often recording the 'secundo folio', *i.e.* the first word on the *second* leaf of a manuscript. This would necessarily be different in every case, and provided a ready means of identifying books containing identical texts, such as Bibles and service-books.

[3] Cf. Santifaller, *Beiträge zur Geschichte der Beschreibstoffe im Mittelalter, mit besonderer Berücksichtigung der päpstlichen Kanzlei*, 1953, pp. 164–5. Pagination does not begin to reappear until the latter part of the twelfth century.

[4] Cf. W. Wattenbach, *Das Schriftwesen im Mittelalter*, 3rd ed., 1896, pp. 150–74.

[5] The general principle, so far as there is one, seems to be that anything intended for continuous or repeated reading or reference was invariably in codex form. This includes literary and scientific works of all kinds, monastic chartularies, collections of statutes, law-books, etc. On the other hand there are certain specialised categories of rolls, such as Rolls of Arms or Mortuary Rolls which are invariably in roll form although they could just as well have been written in codices. Outside the great series of rolls produced by central government, the most prolific source of rolls in England are Court Rolls, the records of manorial courts, which have survived in vast numbers and which continued to be engrossed on rolls down to the middle of the seventeenth century. According to L. Santifaller, *op. cit.*, p. 183, papal records were still being kept on rolls in the third century A.D., but were probably transferred to codices in the fourth century.

[6] The roll also survived to a considerable extent in the East in the liturgy of the

The relevance of medieval practice to the present investigation is that it casts serious doubt on the validity of many of the practical arguments in favour of the codex. For instance, although a certain number of medieval rolls are written on both sides, an even greater number are not, and this indicates that there was no special desire to make the maximum use of the writing material, either by using the back of the roll or by adopting the codex form. Similarly, medieval clerks appear to have coped successfully with all the much-stressed difficulties of locating a particular passage, re-rolling the roll after use, and so on. It is, moreover, possible that, at any rate for the medieval user, the roll may have seemed to offer some positive advantages. One is its flexibility, since extra membranes can readily be sewn on if it desired to extend a roll. Again, rolls need no binding and have survived for many centuries without them, whereas a codex must have some form of binding, if only to hold the quires together, and binding has próbably always been a skilled occupation, involving expense and, in the case of administrative records, delays whilst the binding is being executed.

7. *The effect of conservatism.* One factor which must be borne in mind in assessing the probable impact of the arguments in favour of the codex which we have been discussing is the natural conservatism of professional scribes. Writing a codex involved a variety of problems such as calculating space ahead, laying out sheets and keeping them in the right order, which were non-existent for a scribe writing a roll.[1] And apart from the scribes themselves, all those responsible for the production of books would be inclined to continue as they had always done. Scriptoria and bureaucracies have always tended to crystallize practices, and it is significant that in the Roman Empire the papyrus roll continued to be the normal form for administrative records and accounts for centuries after the codex had replaced it in the field of literature.[2]

Orthodox Church, which was commonly written on parchment rolls, cf. B. Atsalos, *La Terminologie du livre-manuscrit à l'époque byzantine*, 1e partie, 1971, pp. 148–76. For the question whether these and other rolls are a direct survival from the rolls of the ancient world see G. Cavallo, 'La genesi dei rotoli liturgici Beneventani alla luce del fenomeno storico-librario in occidente ed oriente', *Miscellanea in memoria di G. Cencetti*, 1973, pp. 213–29. See also E. G. Turner, *Typology*, pp. 50–1 and references there given.

[1] On these problems see E. G. Turner, *Typology*, pp. 73–4.

[2] A present-day example of conservatism may be quoted here. In the British House of Lords new peers are required to sign a parchment roll called the Test Roll. This roll,

8. *Conclusions.* We have now to consider the extent to which the foregoing arguments might have influenced the early Christians in their choice of the codex. In contrast to the slow and piecemeal process by which the codex ousted the roll in secular literature, the Christian adoption of the codex seems to have been instant and universal. This is all the more striking because we would have expected the earliest Christians, whether Jew or Gentile, to be strongly prejudiced in favour of the roll by upbringing, education and environment. The motivation for their adoption of the codex must therefore have been something overwhelmingly powerful, and certainly none of the reasons considered above appears capable of producing such an effect. We must therefore seek alternative explanations. Two different hypotheses will be here discussed, although neither can be claimed as more than tentative.

begun in 1675, has now grown to 30 membranes with a total length of 36.5 metres, making it very cumbersome to consult. It was proposed, on 5 May 1981, to replace it with a register in book form, but the proposal was negatived without a vote.

10

THE CHRISTIAN ADOPTION OF THE CODEX:
TWO HYPOTHESES

I F – which is by no means certain – the papyrus codex was a development from the parchment notebook, we have first to consider where the parchment notebook itself originated. We have already seen strong reasons for thinking that it was of Roman origin, and these are supported by the fact that the earliest known examples of the parchment codex, the codices mentioned by Martial and discussed above, were Roman, while the very word codex is Latin and has no Greek equivalent.[1] Conversely, there is no trace of the parchment notebook being used for literary purposes in the only Eastern country for which we have adequate evidence, namely Egypt. All this suggests that we should look to Rome for the ultimate origin of the papyrus codex and its adoption by Christians. How did this come about? If we accept the common hypothesis that the Gospel of Mark was the first to be written down, an explanation may be forthcoming. Early tradition records that Mark reduced to writing his own or Peter's reminiscences during the latter's lifetime or, according to some

---

[1] It is remarkable that the Greek language never developed a specific word to designate the codex form. It is true that the Latin *codex* was transliterated as κῶδιξ, but this always possessed a certain official, governmental or legal connotation (cf. Atsalos, *op. cit.*, pp. 143–4): e.g. in the proceedings of the Council of Chalcedon (A.D. 451), where ἀπὸ κώδικος ἀνέγνω = *ex codice recitavit* in the Latin version, of reading from a register of Imperial letters. By this time βιβλίον itself had already come to imply a codex, and was so translated in the Latin version of the *Acta*: cf. L. Santifaller, *op. cit.*, p. 172, 'in der lateinischen Übersetzung wird für βιβλίον in der Regel das Wort *codex*...gebraucht'. The nearest approach to a Greek term for *codex* seems to have been the word σωμάτιον, cf. St Basil, *Ep.* 395, where it is used for a parchment codex in contradistinction to ἐν χάρτῃ i.e. in a (papyrus) roll; and *Ep.* 231, where Basil writes ἐν χάρτῃ while his correspondent Amphilochius prefers to write ἐν σωματίῳ. It should be noted that σωμάτιον by itself could designate either a parchment or a papyrus codex. This is clear from Constantine's well-known order to Eusebius to manufacture fifty copies of the Bible, σωμάτια, specifying that they should be ἐν διφθέραις. Cf. also for its use with no reference to the material Porphyry, *Vit. Plot.* 25. It is significant that the word, the basic meaning of which echoes the Latin *corpus*, expresses the collective or comprehensive nature of the format, and thus provides an indication of why it was adopted.

authorities, shortly after his death,[1] to meet the demands of those who had heard Peter preach. Peter's auditors, whether Jews or Gentiles, would be accustomed to use wax tablets or parchment notebooks for their accounts, for legal and official business, and perhaps for correspondence. It would therefore have been natural for Mark to use the parchment notebook for a work intended to be copied in the same format for a limited and specialist readership, but not to be published as the ancient world understood publication. That Mark's original manuscript was in codex form is independently suggested by the text of the Gospel itself. If the Gospel as we have it is incomplete, as it was clearly thought to be in the ancient world, the loss of the ending is much more intelligible if the manuscript was a codex, since the outermost leaves of a codex are the most exposed to damage, in complete contrast to the last column of a roll, which being in the interior of the manuscript when rolled up is the best protected.[2]

A late tradition, preserved by Eusebius and Jerome,[3] associates Mark with the foundation of the Church of Alexandria, and the connections of this Church, when it emerges into the light of history, are with the West rather than the East.[4] If the Gospel of Mark, in the form of the parchment notebook postulated above, had reached Egypt, it is likely that it would have been copied on papyrus, so much more readily available than parchment, and the papyrus codex might thus have been created.

The foregoing is the hypothesis put forward in the predecessor of the present work,[5] but it must be admitted that the arguments

[1] For a recent discussion of the evidence see J. A. T. Robinson, *Redating the New Testament*, 1976, pp. 107 sq.

[2] On the question whether the conclusion (and also the beginning?) of the Gospel has been lost see C. F. D. Moule, *The Birth of the New Testament*, 3rd ed., 1981, p. 131, n. 1 and references there given. A recent addition to the evidence for the text having broken off at xvi. 8 is the Barcelona codex of Mark in Sahidic (fifth cent.), which omits the final twelve verses. It has also been suggested that the so-called 'Great Omission', whereby Luke, in his use of Mark, skips from Mark vi. 44 to viii. 26 might have been due to the loss of a leaf or two in the manuscript Luke was using, cf. C. C. McCown, *Harvard Theological Review*, 34, 1941, pp. 240-1.

[3] Cf. B. M. Metzger, *The Early Versions of the New Testament*, Part I, Chapter II, Section 1: *The Introduction of Christianity into Egypt and the Translation of the New Testament*, where it is pointed out (p. 99, n. 2) that Eusebius himself describes the report as based only on hearsay.

[4] Cf. Roberts, *op. cit.*, p. 59. The statement there that letters on the date of Easter were exchanged between the churches of Rome and Alexandria in the later second century is incorrect, there being no evidence for this earlier than the third century.

[5] Pp. 187-9.

against it are formidable. In the first place it is hard to see why the notebook format should have been retained in conjunction with a writing material, namely papyrus, not at that time commonly used for such a purpose. The assumption would have to be made that Mark's original manuscript, or copies of it in the same notebook format, already enjoyed a measure of authority when they first reached Egypt, and that the codex format itself thus acquired a symbolic value, not least because it stood out in sharp contrast both to the Jewish Roll of the Law and to the pagan book; and that for these reasons when it came, inevitably in Egypt, to be copied on papyrus, the codex format was preserved.

A second objection is that the obscurity of the early history of the Church of Alexandria makes it difficult to believe that it could have imposed this novel form on other churches.[1] Either Rome or Antioch would have been more likely to have been able to exert such influence. Nor does the fact that the fortunes of discovery have brought to light early Christian codices from Egypt and virtually none from anywhere else prove that the papyrus codex was of Egyptian origin. Moreover, the suggestion that it was the Gospel of Mark which provided the inspiration or the codex is itself difficult to accept. Despite the fact that there is more detailed tradition relating to the date and circumstances of composition of the Gospel of Mark than there is for any of the others (though in this early tradition there is no allusion to Alexandria), this is the very Gospel which has been described as the 'least read and esteemed in the early Church'.[2] Not only is this so in the early Church generally, but in Egypt in particular, in spite of the alleged association of Mark with the See of Alexandria, no manuscript of the second Gospel earlier than the fourth century has so far been discovered there, with the single exception of the Chester Beatty codex of the Four Gospels and Acts. This position contrasts sharply with eleven copies of John, nine of Matthew, and four of Luke from the same first three centuries.[3] The Coptic evidence makes it plain that this cannot be explained as an accident of survival: in Coptic manuscripts of the fourth century

---

[1] On the obscurity of the early Alexandrian church, and possible reasons for this see Roberts, *op. cit.*, pp. 49–51, 71.

[2] J. A. T. Robinson, *op. cit.*, p. 107; see also Von Campenhausen, *op. cit.*, p. 171, n. 112.

[3] Roberts, *op. cit.*, p. 59, n. 5 and p. 61.

there are 60 quotations from Matthew, 15 from Luke, 15 from John, and none from Mark.[1] A Gospel which was so largely ignored, and of which the original manuscript was in all probability so neglected that it lost its final leaf, is unlikely to have set the standard for the Christian book.

Before we consider a different hypothesis to account for the Christian use of the codex, another innovation in the production of Christian manuscripts deserves attention in case the origin of the one throws light on that of the other. This is the use of the so-called *nomina sacra*, contractions marked by a suprascript line of certain divine names and words, particularly θεός, κύριος, Ἰησοῦς and Χριστός.[2] This, like the exclusive employment of the codex form, is strictly a Christian usage unknown to Jewish or pagan manuscripts, and since its existence is taken for granted in a reference in the Epistle of Barnabas it must go back if not to the Apostolic, at least to the Sub-Apostolic Age.[3] It poses the question whether the adoption of the codex and the invention of the system of *nomina sacra* should be regarded as two independent innovations (possibly originating in different areas of the Christian world) or whether there is some connection between them. The possibility of such a connection was first raised by T. C. Skeat in 1969, who wrote: 'The significant fact is that the introduction of the *nomina sacra* seems to parallel very closely the adoption of the papyrus codex; and it is remarkable that those developments should have taken place at almost the same time as the great outburst of activity among Jewish scholars which led to the standardisation of the Hebrew Bible. It is no less remarkable that they seem to indicate a degree of organisation, of conscious planning, and uniformity of practice among the Christian communities which we have hitherto had little reason to suspect, and which throw a new light on the early history of the Church.'[4] It may be further noted that, whether or not this was the intention, *nomina sacra* share the same characteristic with the codex of differentiating Christian from both Jewish and pagan books.

---

[1] The figures are those of Th. Lefort in *Muséon*, 66, 1953, pp. 16 sq., quoted in Roberts, *op. cit.*, p. 61, n. 4.

[2] For the origin and significance of *nomina sacra* see ibid, pp. 26–48.

[3] On the date of the Epistle of Barnabas see now J. A. T. Robinson, *op. cit.*, pp. 313–19, who claims that there is nothing in the Epistle which could not have been written *circ.* A.D. 75, and would himself place it not long after the fall of Jerusalem.

[4] *The Cambridge History of the Bible*, vol. 2, pp. 72–3.

The case for a common origin of the two innovations is *prima facie* strong, and if it is accepted, the beginnings of the Christian codex cannot be associated with Rome and the West (the hypothesis which has been discussed above), since the earliest Latin manuscripts either do not employ *nomina sacra* at all, or do so in an uncertain or irregular fashion.[1] Alexandria would likewise seem to be ruled out in view of the obscurity of the early Egyptian Church referred to above. If these two areas are excluded, there remain only two early Christian churches having sufficient authority to devise such innovations and impose them on Christendom generally, namely Jerusalem and Antioch.

The claims of Jerusalem have been considered elsewhere,[2] but so far only in connection with the *nomina sacra*. We have now to consider the codex as well, and if the link between *nomina sacra* and the codex is valid, and Jerusalem is posited as their place of dual origin, this must have taken place before the outbreak of the Jewish War in A.D. 66 and the flight of the Christian community, whereas in the case of Antioch no such time factor applies. It is, however, not necessary to think of Jerusalem and Antioch as mutually exclusive. Owing to the close links between them, either or both of these innovations might have taken place through joint consultation between the two Churches.[3]

The claims of Antioch[4] for at least some part in the origin of both *nomina sacra* and the codex are strong. It was one of the principal places where Jewish Christians, dispersed from Jerusalem after Stephen's death, sought refuge,[5] and where some of them, Jews from Cyprus and Cyrene (and thus likely to possess

[1] Roberts, *op. cit.*, pp. 43–4.
[2] Roberts, *op. cit.*, pp. 45–6.
[3] In objection to Antioch as the source, or at any rate the sole source of *nomina sacra* it might be urged that *nomina sacra* are unknown in Syriac manuscripts. This, however, seems to be due to the nature of the Syriac language and script. Dr S. P. Brock has kindly pointed out to us that whereas in Greek such forms as $\overline{κc}$ and $\overline{θc}$ are not liable to confusion or misinterpretation, the hypothetical Syriac equivalents (i.e. taking the first and last letters of each word) would be very awkward, *viz.* m' from *mry'* = Lord, and '' from *'lh'* = God, while m' would also be indistinguishable from m' = when, and could also represent the first and last letters of *mšyḥ'* = Messiah. In fact, when *mšyḥ'* does eventually (in medieval manuscripts only) get abbreviated, the system is quite different, *mš* or *mšy* being employed.
[4] For Christianity at Antioch see Glanville Downey, *A History of Antioch in Syria*, 1961, Chapter II: The Christian Community at Antioch from Apostolic times to A.D. 284, and Jean Lassus, 'Antioche à l'époque romaine: Christianisme' in *Aufstieg und Niedergang der römischen Welt*, II. 8, pp. 88–94.
[5] Acts of the Apostles xi. 19.

a knowledge of Greek) preached the Gospel to the Greek-speaking section of the local population.[1] More important, it was in this centre of Greek culture that the breakthrough of the mission to the Gentiles took place. The missionaries to the Gentiles would have needed Greek manuscripts, initially perhaps only of the Septuagint. Obviously these manuscripts, intended for Gentile consumption, cannot have made use of the Hebrew tetragram for the Name of God, and the necessity to find an alternative may have led to the invention of the *nomina sacra*.[2] But we still have to explain the apparently simultaneous emergence of the codex. We know from Jewish sources[3] that while the Oral Law, the Mishnah, could not be formally committed to writing, isolated decisions or rabbinic sayings might be, and were, written down either on tablets (πίνακες) or on what the Mishnah calls 'small private rolls'. Since Jewish children, like Gentile children, started their education on tablets and continued to use them for memoranda, these would have been familiar everyday objects. A decision quoted in the Mishnah,[4] said to be not later than the middle of the second century, mentions three kinds of tablets, those filled with wax, those with a polished surface (like the ivory tablets of the Romans) and those of papyrus, of which, however, only the second fulfilled the ceremonial requirements. There was a large Jewish community in Antioch from Hellenistic times onwards, and tablets of the kinds just mentioned, including tablets of papyrus, would have been in common use amongst the Jews there. It is possible, therefore, that papyrus tablets were used to record the Oral Law as pronounced by Jesus, and that these tablets might have developed into a primitive form of codex. To the records of these *logia* might have been added an account of the Passion, and the way would be clear for the production of a Proto-Gospel.[5]

[1] Acts of the Apostles xi. 20.　　[2] Roberts, *op. cit.*, pp. 34–5.

[3] For this account of Jewish writing habits we are greatly indebted to S. Lieberman, *Hellenism in Jewish Palestine*, 1950, Appendix III, 'Jewish and Christian Codices' (pp. 203 sq.). It may further be noted that in writing the Oral Law on a tablet the form itself would indicate that no real publication was intended, whereas to publish in the form of a roll would be regarded as a transgression of the Law. On publication and the Oral Law see Lieberman, *op. cit.*, pp. 84 sq.

[4] *Kelim*, xxiv. 7 (*The Mishnah*, trans. H. Danby, 1933, p. 639). For the date see Lieberman, *op. cit.*, p. 203.

[5] Various theories have been propounded, suggesting that some, or possibly all, of the Canonical Gospels, and Acts, were written at Antioch, but none can be regarded as proved or even probable; perhaps the strongest case for an Antiochene – or at any rate Syrian – origin is that of the Gospel of Matthew.

Once the Jewish War began, the dominating position of Antioch as the metropolis of Christianity in the Greek-speaking world would have been unchallenged, and any development of the tablet into the codex is most likely to have taken place here, thus laying the foundation of the city as a centre of Biblical scholarship. If the first work to be written on a papyrus codex was a Gospel, it is easy to understand that the codex rapidly became the sole format for the Christian scriptures, given the authority that a Gospel would carry.

Against this, it could be argued that the Jews equally used tablets for recording the Oral Law, but in no case did this usage develop into the codex. On the other hand, the use of the roll in Judaism was so rooted in tradition and prescribed by the Law that such a development would have been impossible. The Christians, however, would have had no such inhibitions, and to them the adoption of a form of book which like the *nomina sacra* would have differentiated them from both Jews and pagans, as already noted, might have constituted an additional attraction.

If the foregoing hypothesis is correct, it follows that the parchment notebook (*membranae*) can have played very little part in the invention of the Christian papyrus codex. It is true that St Paul used parchment note-books (2 Tim. iv. 13), and a second-century papyrus letter from Egypt (P. Petaus 30) mentions the purchase of some μεμβράναι, but evidence to link these references with the Christian papyrus codex is entirely lacking. We have already seen (p. 29), and shall see again (p. 71) that the supposed priority of the parchment codex over the papyrus codex is far from proved even in the field of pagan literature, and in the case of Christian manuscripts the theory is even less convincing. It is indeed by no means easy to find an example of a Christian codex on parchment as early as the third century.[1]

---

[1] One of the earliest Christian parchment codices would appear to be a page of Acts, P. Berlin. Inv. 11765 = van Haelst 479, which is assigned by Roberts to the second–third century. E. G. Turner, however, in *Typology*, under number NT Parch 76, dates it fourth century on pp. 29, 159. In the 'Detailed List of Early Parchment Codices' in *Typology*, p. 39 (cf. also p. 94) there are no Christian items ascribed to the second–third century. Five are ascribed to the third century, *viz.*:

1 Romans. NT Parch 82 (van Haelst 495)
2 2 John. NT Parch 107 (van Haelst 555)
3 Acts of Peter. NT Apocrypha 13 (van Haelst 603)
4 Genesis. OT 2 (van Haelst 5)
5 Tobit. OT 186 (van Haelst 82)

To sum up, although neither of the two hypotheses discussed above is capable of proof, the second is decidedly the more plausible. One final point to be considered is the date at which the Christians may be presumed to have adopted the codex, or rather the date by which general agreement was reached in the Church that the codex was the only acceptable format for the Scriptures. Neither hypothesis provides any chronological background. So far as the first is concerned, if the Gospel of Mark provided the ultimate model, we do not know when the Gospel was written, when copies of it could have reached Alexandria, or how long it would have taken for papyrus to replace parchment as the writing material. The second hypothesis is equally unproductive. If Jerusalem was involved in the adoption of the codex, this must have been, as noted above, before A.D. 66; but if Antioch was also involved, a later date is equally possible.

The only hard evidence thus remains that of the manuscripts themselves. We have seen that there are a number of Christian papyrus codices dating from the second century, including at least one which is agreed to be not later than A.D. 150. These manuscripts are all, so far as we can judge, provincial productions, and it is thus in the highest degree unlikely that they are the earliest codices ever produced. All in all, it is impossible to believe that the Christian adoption of the codex can have taken place any later than *circ*. A.D. 100 (it may, of course have been earlier); and this date will be assumed in the following Section.

But concerning these five items some reservations must be made. No. 1 is dated ?iii, *i.e.* third century with a query, on p. 160. No. 2 is dated 'iii ed.; E.G.T. iv?' on p. 163. No. 3 was dated early fourth century by the original editors (and by H. J. M. Milne). No. 4 is possibly Jewish, cf. Roberts, *op. cit.*, pp. 33–4, 77. No 5 is dated third–fourth century by Cavallo.

11

THE CHRISTIAN CODEX AND THE CANON OF SCRIPTURE

IT has sometimes been suggested that the adoption of the codex by the early Christians in some way influenced the development of the Canon of Scripture. No ancient writer alludes to this, and there is no direct evidence, so whatever can be said on the subject must necessarily be conjectural.

As regards the Christian Bible as a whole, any possible influence of the codex on its contents can be immediately dismissed. Manuscripts of the entire Greek Bible are excessively rare at any period, and in any case the history of the Old Testament Canon, depending predominantly upon the Jewish Canon, is quite different from that of the New.

Even in the case of the New Testament as an entity it may be doubted whether the existence of the codex has ever had any effect upon the Canon. Manuscripts of the complete New Testament in Greek are by no means common. Of the 2,646 minuscule manuscripts listed by Kurt Aland in his *Kurzgefasste Liste der griechischen Handschriften des Neuen Testaments*, 1963, pp. 61–202, only 56 contain the New Testament complete, while a further 136 contain the New Testament *minus* the Apocalypse, which the Eastern Churches long regarded with suspicion. The same picture is broadly true of the Latin[1] and other early versions. Any influence of the codex on the contents of the New Testament must therefore have been on smaller groups, particularly the Gospels and the Pauline Epistles.

To take the Gospels, if the establishment of the Four-Gospel Canon is linked in some way with the adoption of the codex, there are three possibilities. Either the Canon came first, and favoured the adoption of the codex, which made it possible to include all four Gospels in a single volume; or the adoption of the codex came first, and realisation of its possibilities favoured the establishment of the Four-Gospel Canon; or, whether by chance or design, both

---

[1] On Latin manuscripts of the complete Bible – 'Pandects' – see B. M. Metzger, *The Early Versions of the New Testament*, p. 336, n. 1.

developments took place simultaneously, without either necessarily influencing the other.

We have already seen that the adoption of the codex cannot
be dated later than *circ.* A.D. 100, and much therefore depends
upon the date to be assigned to the establishment of the Four-
Gospel Canon, or at any rate whether this took place before or
after A.D. 100. Unfortunately there is at present no general
agreement on the date or circumstances in which the Canon
emerged. The latest writer on the subject, Hans von Campenhausen, in *The Formation of the Christian Bible*, 1972, would place
the emergence of the Canon between the time of Justin and that
of Irenaeus (pp. 171–2), *i.e.* between *circ.* 160 and *circ.* 185, adding
'to define the date more precisely than this is not possible'. His
reason for this is that 'the Four-Gospel canon was not a conscious
creation, "constructed" at one blow, nor was it disseminated from
a single centre. Its formation was gradual and the result of earlier
presuppositions, and it was in the end universally accepted.' As
for the circumstances, he takes the view that the Canon came into
being either by direct reaction to the activities of Marcion or,
which he thinks more likely, because Marcion created a situation
in which the Church was obliged to define what was authoritative
and authentic. Elsewhere, however, he seems to allow a rather
wider span of years for the emergence of the Canon, as when he
refers to 'when the beginnings of the Four-Gospel canon are
placed, as they must be, only in the second half of the second
century' (*op. cit.*, p. 238, n. 156).

According to Irenaeus the Four-Gospel Canon is something
divinely established and consonant with the forces of nature, and
the date of *circ.* 185 can thus safely be taken as the *terminus ante
quem* for the creation of the Canon. But it is by no means so certain
that the age of Justin provides us with a *terminus post quem*.
Professor Moule, for example, leaves it open whether the Four-
Gospel Canon is earlier or later than Marcion (*circ.* 140): 'Did that
interesting heretic find four Gospels already recognized together
by about A.D. 140, and did he deliberately drop off Matthew,
Mark, and John (as well as the unacceptable parts of Luke)? Or
was it rather that the catholic Church, after seeing what havoc
Marcion wrought by his one-sided use of documents, brought the
four Gospels together to restore the balance and make a fourfold
harmony? This is the same problem as confronts us for the whole

New Testament canon: was Marcion's the first canon, and is the orthodox canon the catholic Church's subsequent reply? Or did Marcion play fast and loose with an already existing canon? There is at present no conclusive evidence for the existence of a pre-Marcionite catholic canon. Marcion may have been the catalyst we have already hinted at. We cannot be certain' (*The Birth of the New Testament*, 3rd ed., 1981, pp. 257–8).

In this climate of uncertainty it is very difficult to trace any possible link between the Four-Gospel Canon and the adoption of the codex.[1] All that can be said is that so far at least no critic has suggested a date for the creation of the Canon as early as A.D. 100; and we may thus reach the tentative conclusion that the adoption of the codex pre-dated the Four-Gospel Canon. If this is so, we have now to consider whether the Canon was influenced by the existence of the codex.

Pre-existence of the codex was certainly not essential for the creation of the Canon. The Jews, after all, created their own canon of the Old Testament without any benefit of the codex, and no doubt the Christian Church could have decided upon the Four-Gospel Canon irrespective of whether at the time the Four Gospels were circulating as four rolls, four codices, or one codex. One area in which it has been claimed the codex exercised a decisive effect is the canonical order of the Gospels. As Campenhausen puts it: 'Any publication which established a fixed sequence of gospels is conceivable only as from the start in the form of a codex' (*op. cit.*, p. 173). But against this is the evidence of variations in sequence, notably the so-called 'Western Order' of Matthew, John, Luke, Mark which is also found in the fourth-century Freer Gospels, a manuscript almost certainly of Egyptian origin, while Campenhausen himself points out that although Irenaeus in discussing the origins of the Gospels treats them in the

---

[1] The most detailed proposal to link the adoption of the codex form with the Four-Gospel Canon is that of G. Rudberg, *Neutestamentlicher Text und Nomina Sacra*, Uppsala, 1915, pp. 36–46. Accepting the thesis of Hermann von Soden that his three families of Gospel manuscripts, I, H and K, all derived from a single I–H–K archetype, Rudberg concluded that this archetype implied a codex, since a single roll could not contain all four Gospels: cf. *op. cit.*, p. 36, 'Diese technische Einheit der Evangelien, mit dem I–H–K Text, kann nicht eine Rolle gewesen sein und auch nicht mehrere... Wir müssen ein Buch, ein Codex annehmen'. The adoption of the codex and the establishment of the Four-Gospel Canon were thus intimately connected and each presupposes the other. However, von Soden's theories have not found acceptance, and in any case the position has been radically altered by subsequent discoveries.

canonical sequence (apparently because he believed this was their chronological order), he elsewhere always uses the order Matthew, Luke, Mark, John (*op. cit.*, p. 195, n. 243).

But perhaps the strongest argument against any definite link between the Four-Gospel Canon and the codex is the extent to which, both during and after the second century, Gospels continued to circulate individually or in smaller groups or in conjuction with other books of the Bible, and that too not only in Greek but in the Versions also. Examples from the fourth century onwards are given by Zahn,[1] but there are plenty of earlier date. The earliest extant Gospel manuscript, the Rylands St John (P 52) probably never contained more than that Gospel (see below), as certainly was the case with the somewhat later Bodmer St John (P 66) and the third-century P 5, a bifolium consisting of conjoint leaves from the beginning and end of a single-quire codex of the same Gospel, while another notable example is the fourth-century codex of John in Sub-Achmimic from Qau. For groups of less than four Gospels we have the Bodmer Luke and John (P 75), the codex of Matthew and Luke divided between Paris, Oxford and Barcelona (P 4 + P 64 + P 67), or the fifth-century Barcelona codex of Luke and Mark (in that order) in the Sahidic version.

Despite such negative results, it is of some interest to speculate whether in the second century it would have been feasible to include all four Gospels within a single codex. There is no doubt that this would have been technically possible, if we compare the example of the second-century codex of the *Republic* of Plato discussed below. The *Republic* contains 11,846 στίχοι, whereas the Four Gospels, according to the calculations of Rendel Harris (using the text of Westcott and Hort and making allowances for *nomina sacra*) contain only 8,345 στίχοι. The Plato codex is, however, written in an exceptionally small hand, unlike that of early Christian manuscripts, and the available evidence from second-century codices of the Gospels is not favourable to the existence of a Four-Gospel codex. The most extensive second-century Christian codex is the Chester Beatty Numbers and Deuteronomy,[2] which contained 108 leaves (= 216 pages). A

[1] *Geschichte des neutestamentlichen Kanons*, i, 1881, p. 60.
[2] In the stichometry of Nicephorus (Migne, *Patr. Gr.* 100, col. 1055) Numbers and Deuteronomy together comprise 6630 στίχοι.

Four-Gospel manuscript written in the same style and format would have contained about 135 leaves (= 270 pages). The Bodmer Luke and John (P 75) originally consisted of 72 leaves (= 144 pages), and the addition of Matthew and Mark would have required at least an additional 60 leaves, making a total of 132 leaves (= 264 pages). The Paris–Oxford–Barcelona codex of Matthew and Luke mentioned above is very fragmentary, but the remains of Luke indicate that the Gospel would have filled about 44 leaves (= 88 pages), and on this basis the Four Gospels would have occupied a total of 144 leaves (= 288 pages). As will be seen, all these figures are considerably larger than those for any second-century codex at present known.

In the next century the Chester Beatty Gospels and Acts (P 45) originally contained 110 leaves (= 220 pages), and this was achieved by the use of a larger page (about 25.5×20 cm), giving a larger written area (about 19×16 cm), together with a smaller script than in most of the second-century codices. For the present, therefore, a second-century codex of all four Gospels seems unlikely; and there is much to be said for Campenhausen's conclusion: 'the fact that Irenaeus and the Muratorian canon regard the fourfold gospel as a spiritual unity is a theological phenomenon and nothing to do with book production' (op. cit., p. 174).

Hitherto we have spoken only of the Gospels. Of the remainder of the New Testament, the most obvious group which might have been influenced by the codex is the Pauline Epistles. These form a body considerably shorter than the Gospels (5,095 στίχοι according to Rendel Harris),[1] so a codex containing all of them would have been proportionately more feasible in the second century, as the Chester Beatty codex shows that it was in the third. But there is no evidence whatsoever to indicate that the codex played any part in their selection or circulation.[2]

[1] Op. cit., pp. 38–9; this figure includes the Pastoral Epistles and Hebrews.

[2] For theories of the creation of the Pauline canon, and the possible influence of Marcion's selection of Pauline Epistles see von Campenhausen, op. cit., pp. 176 ff., Moule, op. cit., pp. 258–66. E. J. Goodspeed and John Knox, who suggested that the collection was the work of the slave Onesimus, placed the event soon after A.D. 85, while according to G. Zuntz the archetype of the Pauline corpus was produced, possibly in Alexandria, about A.D. 100 (references in Moule, loc. cit.).

12

THE CODEX IN NON-CHRISTIAN LITERATURE

WE have attempted to explain why the early – if not indeed the earliest – Christians adopted the codex form for their Scriptures to the virtual exclusion of the roll. We have now to face the even more difficult problem of finding an explanation for the transition from the roll to the codex in the realm of non-Christian literature. As the figures in Section 7 will have shown, this was no sudden revolution but a slow, irreversible drift from one form to the other which required several centuries for completion.

At first sight the most obvious explanation would seem to be the influence of current Christian practice. Certainly after A.D. 300, and possibly even some decades earlier, the sight of Christian codices must have been familiar to a large and ever-increasing proportion of all classes of the population, and we may imagine that the final triumph of Christianity would have provided greatly increased motivation to adopt the Christian model. However, the figures just mentioned show clearly that although the codex makes only a modest showing among non-Christian manuscripts of the second century A.D., their number is nevertheless appreciable, and that at a time when the possibility of any Christian influence can be firmly excluded.

At this point we must consider the latest discussion of the origin of the codex, by Professor G. Cavallo in the volume *Libri, Editori e Pubblico nel mondo antico: Guida storica e critica*, Roma, 1975, pp. xix–xxii, 83–6. He begins by referring to the various practical advantages which have been claimed for the codex, and which have been considered in detail in Section 9 above – cheapness, compactness, ease of reference, etc., – but insists that they can have played only a minor or complementary role in the process. He then develops his own theory. Admitting the priority of the Christian codex, he argues that the early Christians came from the lower strata of society, among whom a book would have been a rarity, and that among such classes, whether Christian or not, the codex-form note-book would have been a familiar object used for memoranda, commercial transactions and the like. Such literature as these classes possessed would not have been the classics but either popular romances like the *Phoinikika* of Lollianus, itself a second century codex, or, in the case of artisans, works of a technical or practical character. These classes would have not been merely indifferent to, but actually antagonistic to the roll, a form associated in their minds with an aristocratic élite. As these same circles developed into an increasingly powerful middle class, their preferences would have gradually dominated the book-production industry, and eventually even the aristocracy would have had to conform and adopt the codex.

Persuasively though the case is argued by Professor Cavallo, it must be admitted that it is difficult to find any supporting evidence. The theory that the early Christians were drawn predominantly from the lower classes, and that this would have favoured their adoption of the codex recalls the position taken up by Wilhelm Schubart sixty years ago (*Das Buch bei den Griechen und Römern*, 2nd ed., 1921, pp. 119 ff.: *Der Codex, das Buch der Ärmeren*).[1] Of course the numerical majority of Christians at this, or indeed any age would have come from the lower classes,[2] but it by no means follows that it would have been they who would have decided such important questions as the format of their Scriptures. And it is surely an exaggeration to say that to such persons a book would have been a rarity. Certainly it is difficult to believe that any inhabitant of, say, Oxyrhynchus can never have caught sight of a book. The roll itself must have been even more familiar from its massive use not only in official circles such as the army, the courts and the bureaucracy down to local government level, but also by private businessmen for their accounts and records.

---

[1] The title itself is not original, being taken from Birt's *Abriss*, p. 351.

[2] This is a widely-held belief. Cf., e.g., Cavallo, *op. cit.*, p. xx.: 'a dar vita alle prime comunità cristiane fu una *plebs* senza ruolo economico, politico e intellettuale'. But cf. E. A. Judge, *The Social Pattern of the Christian Groups in the first century*, 1960, p. 60: 'Far from being a socially depressed group, then if the Corinthians are at all typical, the Christians were dominated by a socially pretentious section of the population of the big cities'. Also p. 61: 'Pliny accepted the fact that Christians represented a broad cross-section of society, from Roman citizens downwards, but reserved his surprise, apart from their numbers, in which he is an alarmist, for the ominous fact that the new religion was infecting not merely the cities but the countryside. Until then, however, we may safely regard Christianity as a socially well-backed movement of the great Hellenistic cities'.

The suggestion that there was a kind of distinct sub-culture whose favourite reading was popular romances in codex form is an attractive one, but hard evidence for this is slender. If we analyse the surviving fragments of romances from Egypt we find the following picture:

	Rolls	Codices
1st century	4	0
1st–2nd century	2	0
2nd century	9	2
2nd–3rd century	10	0
3rd century	4	1
Total	29	3

These figures are taken from O. Montevecchi, *La Papirologia*, 1973, pp. 360–3 with some later additions, *viz.* P. Oxy. xxxi. 2539, xlii. 3010, 3011, 3012, and P. Turner 8. The two second century codices are Achilles Tatius, (Pack² no. 3) and the *Phoinikika* of Lollianus already mentioned; the third century codex is again Achilles Tatius (Pack² no. 1).[1]

If we take other types of literature which might reasonably be regarded as popular, one obvious *genre* is the so-called Acts of the Pagan Martyrs or Acta Alexandrinorum. For these texts Montevecchi gives the following figures:

1st century	5
1st–2nd century	0
2nd century	8
2nd–3rd century	8
3rd century	7
Total	28

Every one of these is a roll.

A work which one would have thought was a work of popular literature *par excellence* is the Oracle of the Potter. Of this there

---

[1] At the end of the section 'Romance' Pack² lists other possible romance texts; of the eight antedating the fifth century not one is a codex or opisthograph; one is an ostrakon.

are three manuscripts, one of the second century and two of the third: all are rolls.

Similarly the popular fortune-telling manual known as the Sortes of Astrampsychus has survived in five manuscripts, *viz.* P. Oxy. xii. 1477, P. Oxy. xxxviii. 2832 + xlvii. 3330, xxxviii. 2833, P. Leid. (forthcoming in P. Lugd.-Bat. 24), and P. Oxy. ined. (G. M. Browne, 'A new papyrus codex of the *Sortes Astrampsychi*', *Arktouros: Hellenic Studies presented to Bernard M. W. Knox*...1979, pp. 434–9). The first four all date from the third–fourth century and are all on rolls, notwithstanding the fact that the codex form would have been especially convenient for the consultation of the work. Only the fifth is a codex, and that is the latest of all (late fourth century). Again, although manuals of magic might equally be expected to adopt the codex form, no extant magical codex is earlier than the fourth century; and the same goes for the two known treatises on palmomancy (Pack² no. 2112, 2113).

It will be seen, then, that the attempt to link readers of popular literature with a preference for the codex is not supported by the evidence, at any rate so far as Egypt is concerned, and we have no reason to think that Egypt was untypical in this respect. The further claim that texts of a technical character in codex form formed part of the reading of the artisan class is even more difficult to substantiate. No examples are given, and a search through the list of codices at the end of E. G. Turner's *Typology* does not readily reveal a single example which one might picture in the hands of an artisan. In the present state of knowledge, therefore, both these hypotheses must be regarded as unproved.

Professor Cavallo sums up his position by describing the motivation for the change to the codex as 'pressure from below' (*una spinta dal basso*) and links this with the profound social and economic changes which transformed classical society into the world of Late Antiquity. According to him, the break-up of the fragile equilibrium of the Antonine age led to a progressive sharpening of class divisions, with the social élite, the society of the roll, slowly but steadily shrinking into an ever smaller minority and becoming increasingly alienated from what Professor Cavallo claims to be the new reading public of the middle and lower classes. Such a period of change may well have facilitated the growth in popularity of the codex, but it does not explain it. If Professor Cavallo's thesis is at best not proven, we must search for an alternative, beginning with a list of non-Christian codices which have been, or can be, plausibly assigned to the second century. In this list the items, seventeen in all, are denominated by their Pack² numbers; we have further added the reference numbers in the 'Consolidated List of Codices consulted' in E. G. Turner, *The Typology of the early codex*, together with the notes on dating there given (and which does not always agree with our own).

The first two to be listed have long been well known as among the earliest surviving examples of parchment codices:

1 Pack² 293. Demosthenes, *De falsa legatione*. *Typology* 47 (ii)
2 Pack² 437. Euripides, *Cretans*. *Typology* 80 (ii ?)

The remaining examples apart from no. 16, are all on papyrus:
3 Pack² 3. Achilles Tatius, *Leucippe and Cleitophon*. *Typology* 2 (ii)
4 Pack² 311. Commentary on Demosthenes, *In Aristocratem*. *Typology* 52 (iii E.G.T.; ii ed., C.H.R.)
5 Pack² 645. Homeromanteion + 1801 (Epic Katabasis). *Typology* 107 (ii/iii; ii C.H.R.)
6 Pack² 747. Homer, *Iliad* v. *Typology* 122 (ii/iii E.G.T.)
7 Pack² 868. Homer, *Iliad* ii. *Typology* 139 (ii ed.; iii E.G.T.)
8 Pack² 1362. Pindar, *Paeans*. *Typology* 250 (ii ed., E.G.T.)
9 Pack² 1546. Xenophon, *Cyropaedia*. *Typology* 280 (ii)
10 Pack² 2145. Grammatical manual. *Typology* 356 (iii E.G.T.)
11 Pack² 2155. Grammatical manual. *Typology* 359 (iii E.G.T.)
12 Pack² 2340. Medical treatise. *Typology* 387 (ii ?)
13 Pack² 2355. Medical manual. *Typology* 389 (i–ii – so ed.)
14 P. Oxy. xxx. 2517. Lexicon to Homer. *Typology* 207a (ii)
15 Lollianus, *Phoinikika*. *Typology* 223a (late ii)
16 Plato, *Parmenides*. *Typology* 254 (iii/iv E.G.T.; ii ed.)
17 P. Oxy. xliv. 3157. Plato, *Republic*. *Typology* 255a (ii)

The first and most obvious characteristic of these codices is that they are a very mixed lot – prose and verse, scientific and technical, – and this suggests, as a first conclusion, that it may be a mistake to search for any one cause for the transition from roll to codex in all cases. If we now examine the items in detail, we may begin by considering whether any of these fragments may come from 'one-volume' manuscripts. This would certainly appear to be the case with the last, the *Republic* of Plato. This contains approximately 59 στίχοι to the page, and since the total number of στίχοι in all ten books of the *Republic*, according to the figures for the individual books given by Birt, *Buchwesen*, p. 442, is 11, 846, P. Oxy. 3157, if it contained the entire work, would have been a codex of almost exactly 100 leaves (= 200 pages). The size of the page seems to have been about 13 × 22 cm, and if we take the thickness of the papyrus as 0.3 mm, the hypothetical manuscript would have been a very handy volume measuring 13 × 22 × 3 cm, excluding the binding. By contrast, the contemporary P. Oxy. xlvii 3326, a fragment of a roll of Book VIII of the *Republic*, according to the editor 'probably contained this book and no more; this would make it about seven metres long'. All this suggests that some other manuscripts in the above list may have been one-volume editions. The Xenophon, for instance (no. 9) might have contained the entire *Cyropaedia* (10,817 στίχοι according to Birt, *op. cit.*, p. 441), as was certainly the case with the third-century codex P. Ryl. iii. 549. We may similarly speculate whether the fragment of the *Paeans* (no. 8) came from a complete Pindar, and whether the Achilles Tatius (no. 3) contained the whole of *Leucippe and Cleitophon*.[1]

But this is clearly not the whole of the story. The two grammatical fragments (nos. 10 and 11) suggest a use in education, and if so it may have been the convenience of the codex in exposition that motivated the adoption of the new form. The same reason may explain the presence of the two medical fragments (nos. 12 and 13), if these were used for instruction. The role played by Homer (nos. 6 and 7) in primary education needs no emphasising. Convenience of use might also explain the Homeric lexicon (no. 14) and, in a different context, the fortune-telling Homeromanteion (no. 5). This last makes it all the more surprising that, as noted above, scribes who copied works of fortune-telling, divination and magic signally failed to take advantage of the codex format.

One crucial point must be reiterated here. On pp. 40–1 above we listed thirteen Christian manuscripts in codex form which in our view can be assigned to the second century. We now have seventeen non-Christian manuscripts in codex form which can be similarly dated, and at first sight it might seem that at least in

[1] At a rough estimate the romance ran to about 5500 στίχοι and so could have been contained in quite a small codex.

this century there is no appreciable difference between Christian and non-Christian practice in the use of the codex form. But the backgrounds to these sets of figures are entirely different. The thirteen Christian codices are the only known examples of Christian manuscripts of the second century, if we except two rolls, one of which being written on the verso of a roll is not evidence of the choice of the roll format. The seventeen non-Christian codices, on the other hand, must be balanced against 857 rolls dating from the same period: in other words, codices here amount to only about 2 % of the total, a proportion so small and so constantly confirmed by new discoveries that we are bound to accept that in non-Christian literature of the second century the codex played only a very small – though still not entirely negligible – part.

The foregoing speculations must necessarily remain unproven, but they do suggest strongly that, as already surmised, a variety of different reasons operated in favour of the codex in the non-Christian world. Although Martial's experiments (and perhaps others of which we have no knowledge) do not seem to have had any immediate success, the idea of the codex as an acceptable vehicle for literature maintained a tenuous existence and provided the inspiration for the manuscripts we have been considering. It would seem that the twin advantages of comprehensiveness and convenience were gradually appreciated and that this process, as the figures show, steadily gained momentum during the third century. The triumph of Christianity may well have provided the final impulsion, although it seems likely that even without this the codex would eventually become the victor.

Finally, why did the whole process take so long? As already suggested, sheer conservatism must have played a very large part in delaying the change. Scriptoria are by nature homes of tradition, and the educated reading public which set the standards may have been equally resistant to change. Another factor which has escaped attention, and is difficult for us to appreciate, is that the whole battery of aids to reading and comprehension which the reader of to-day takes for granted – the separation of words, systematic provision of accents and breathings, punctuation, paragraphing, chapter headings, lists of contents, footnotes, indexes, bibliographies, etc. – simply did not exist in the ancient world nor (and this is important) was their absence felt, however indispensable they may seem to us. In just the same way the advantages of the codex (and disadvantages of the roll) may well not have been so apparent to the second-century public and may therefore not have operated so forcefully and speedily in effecting the change as the critic of to-day would expect.

13

EPILOGUE

As will have been seen from the statistics quoted above, the crucial date in the history of the codex is *circ.* A.D. 300, when the codex achieved parity with the roll. Thereafter the use of the roll rapidly diminished. By the fifth century, at least if we may judge from texts found in Egypt, the roll held barely 10 % of the market; and by the sixth it had vanished for ever as a vehicle for literature.

The replacement of the roll by the codex must have had profound effects upon the transmission of literature, but it is not easy to define these effects precisely or to say how they were achieved. In the first place, it is likely that in an increasingly poverty-stricken age, marked by contracting culture and declining literacy, the codex with its greater capacity would have fostered the production of selections of works such as those of the Attic dramatists, or the compilation of epitomes and florilegia. But this subject would require a book to itself. Nor is it easy to say how the actual transmission of texts was affected. It is true that (if we disregard the results of excavation) no single work of ancient literature has survived above ground through the Middle Ages in roll form. But the corollary, that if the codex form had never been devised, the whole of ancient literature would have been lost to us, is less easily demonstrated. Certainly the fact that a work of ancient literature achieved circulation in codex form was no automatic passport to survival. One has only to think of the multitude of works read by Photius in the ninth century (and which must obviously have been codices) and which have subsequently vanished, to appreciate this. And overshadowing everything is the sheer accident of survival, mitigated only by the influence of the schools. If we reflect on the number of works which depend for their text on a very few manuscripts, or even a single exemplar, we can see how difficult it is to assign a precise role to the influence of the codex. On the purely practical level we would offer here two considerations which, if we are correct, may have played a part in enabling the codex to contribute to the survival of ancient literature. Firstly, the superior capacity of the codex, with an average content perhaps six times that of the roll, had the result that, where a manuscript did survive, a much greater volume of text was preserved than would have been the case with a single roll. As a result, works which could be included within a single codex, such as Virgil, are likely to have survived intact, while more voluminous works have reached us in much larger sections than would have been the case if transmission had depended upon the roll: the decads of Livy, for instance, are a good example. Secondly, the roll was particularly susceptible to damage, since despite the use of book-boxes rolls seem to have been frequently shelved without any such covering, and whilst in use were totally exposed to wear and tear. The very construction of the codex, on the other hand, imposed some form of binding, and this gave the contents a hitherto unprecedented and enduring degree of protection.

But all these speculations are for the future. For practical purposes our enquiry ends in the fourth century, and the Codex Sinaiticus (here illustrated), written about the middle of the century, represents the apex of development of the codex. Thereafter, the codex form remained unaltered for more than a thousand years, until the twin developments of paper and printing transformed it into the book of to-day.

LIST OF TEXTS REFERRED TO

PLATES

PLATE I

The Petrie Museum, University College, London, UC 36088, 36089

Inscribed wax tablet, mid third century B.C.: account of expenses incurred on journey in Lower Egypt. Actual measurement of each tablet 9·1 cm × 5·7 cm.

PLATE II

Berlin, Staatlichen Museen, P. Berol. 7358/9

Notebook on thin leather, second century A.D., with notes of labour employed and
payments made. Actual measurements 7·5 cm × 11·8 cm.

PLATE III

Dublin, Chester Beatty Library, Papyrus II, ff. 15r and 90r

Papyrus Codex of the Pauline Epistles, third century A.D.: the conjoint leaves show Romans xi. 24–33 on the left and on the right the end of Philippians and the beginning of Colossians. Actual measurements 19 cm × 30 cm.

PLATE IV

British Library, Add. MS. 34473, art 1

Parchment Codex of Demosthenes, *De Falsa Legatione*, second century A.D.: the plate shows the two pages of a bifolium, slightly reduced, each with two columns to the page. Actual measurement of a page 19 cm × 16.5 cm.

PLATE V

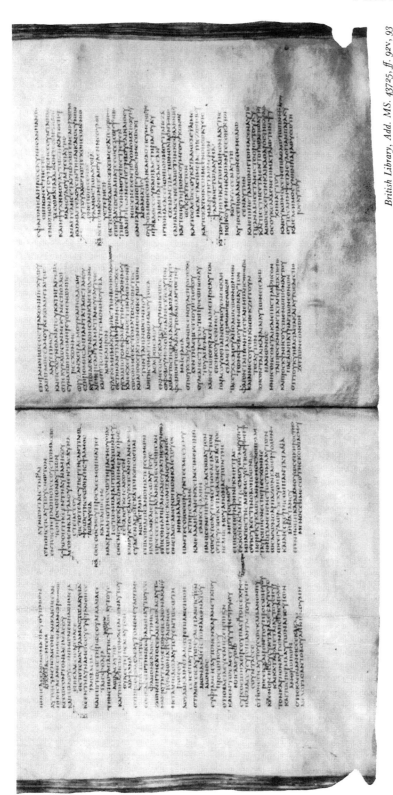

*British Library, Add. MS. 43725, ff. 92*v*, 93*

Parchment Codex of the Bible, Codex Sinaiticus, fourth century A.D.; the bifolium shows in part Psalms xix. 8–xxiii. 5. Actual measurement of a page 37·6 × *c.* 24·7 cm.

PLATE VI

Pontificia Commissione di Archeologia Sacra

Painting of a young man holding an open Codex, from the catacomb of
SS. Peter and Marcellinus, Rome, third century

Printed and bound by CPI Group (UK) Ltd, Croydon, CR0 4YY